TH
WHO
HARNESSED
THE WIND

YOUNG READERS EDITION

William Kamkwamba *and* Bryan Mealer
illustrated by Anna Hymas

PUFFIN BOOKS

PUFFIN BOOKS
An imprint of Penguin Random House LLC
375 Hudson Street
New York, New York 10014

First published in the United States of America by Dial Books for Young Readers,
an imprint of Penguin Group (USA) LLC, 2015
Published by Puffin Books, an imprint of Penguin Random House LLC, 2015

Text copyright © 2015 by William Kamkwamba and Bryan Mealer
Illustrations copyright © 2015 by Anna Hymas

THE LIBRARY OF CONGRESS HAS CATALOGED THE DIAL EDITION AS FOLLOWS:
Kamkwamba, William, date, author.
The boy who harnessed the wind / William Kamkwamba and Bryan Mealer.
—Young readers edition.
pages cm
ISBN 978-0-8037-4080-8 (hardcover)
1. Kamkwamba, William, date—Juvenile literature. 2. Mechanical engineers—Malawi—
Biography—Juvenile literature. 3. Inventors—Malawi—Biography—Juvenile literature.
4. Windmills—Malawi—Juvenile literature. 5. Electric power production—Malawi—
Juvenile literature. 6. Irrigation—Malawi—Juvenile literature. I. Mealer, Bryan. II. Title.

TJ140.K36A3 2015
621.453096897—dc23
2014019191

Puffin Books ISBN 978-0-14-751042-6

13

To my family
–W.K.

CONTENTS

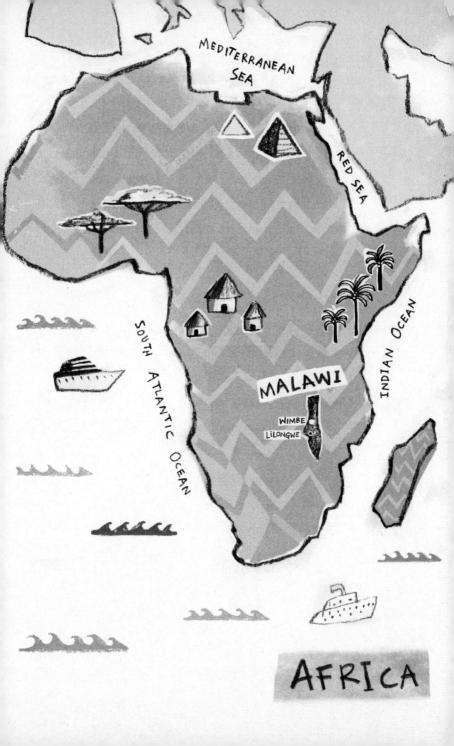

THE
BOY
WHO
HARNESSED
THE
WIND

PROLOGUE

The machine was ready. After so many months of preparation, the work was finally complete: The motor and blades were bolted and secured, the chain was taut and heavy with grease, and the tower stood steady on its legs. The muscles in my back and arms had grown as hard as green fruit from all the pulling and lifting. And although I'd barely slept the night before, I'd never felt so awake. My invention was complete. It appeared exactly as I'd seen it in my dreams.

News of my work had spread far and wide, and now people began to arrive. The traders in the market had watched it rise from a distance and they'd closed up their shops, while the truck drivers left their vehicles on the

1

road. They'd crossed the valley toward my home, and now they gathered under the machine, looking up in wonder. I recognized their faces. These same men had teased me from the beginning, and still they whispered, even laughed.

Let them, I thought. It was time.

I pulled myself onto the tower's first rung and began to climb. The soft wood groaned under my weight as I reached the top, where I stood level with my creation. Its steel bones were welded and bent, and its plastic arms were blackened from fire.

I admired its other pieces: the bottle-cap washers, rusted tractor parts, and the old bicycle frame. Each one told its own story of discovery. Each piece had been lost and then found in a time of fear and hunger and pain. Together now, we were all being reborn.

In one hand I clutched a small reed that held a tiny lightbulb. I now connected it to a pair of wires that dangled from the machine, then prepared for the final step. Down below, the crowd cackled like hens.

"Quiet, everyone," someone said. "Let's see how crazy this boy really is."

Just then a strong gust of wind whistled through the rungs and pushed me into the tower. Reaching over, I unlocked the machine's spinning wheel and watched it begin to turn. Slowly at first, then faster and faster, until the whole tower rocked back and forth. My knees turned to jelly, but I held on.

I pleaded in silence: *Don't let me down.*

Then I gripped the reed and wires and waited for the miracle of electricity. Finally, it came, a tiny flicker in my palm, and then a magnificent glow. The crowd gasped, and the children pushed for a better look.

"It's true!" someone said.

"Yes," said another. "The boy has done it. He has made electric wind!"

CHAPTER ONE

WHEN MAGIC RULED THE WORLD

My name is William Kamkwamba, and to understand the story I'm about to tell, you must first understand the country that raised me. Malawi is a tiny nation in south-eastern Africa. On a map, it appears like a flatworm burrowing its way through Zambia, Mozambique, and Tanzania, looking for a little room. Malawi is often called "The Warm Heart of Africa," which says nothing about its location, but everything about the people who call it home. The Kamkwambas hail from the center of the country, from a tiny village called Masitala, located on the outskirts of the town of Wimbe.

You might be wondering what an African village looks like. Well, ours consists of about ten houses, each one made of mud bricks and painted white. For most of my life, our roofs were made from long grasses that we picked near the swamps, or *dambos* in our Chichewa language. The grasses kept us cool in the hot months, but during the cold nights of winter, the frost crept into our bones and we slept under an extra pile of blankets.

Every house in Masitala belongs to my large extended family of aunts and uncles and cousins. In our house, there was me, my mother and father, and my six sisters, along with some goats and guinea fowl, and a few chickens.

When people hear I'm the only boy among six girls, they often say, *"Eh, bambo"*—which is like saying "Hey, man"—"so sorry for you!" And it's true. The downside to having only sisters is that I often got bullied in school since I had no older brothers to protect me. And my sisters were always messing with my things—especially my tools and inventions—giving me no privacy.

Whenever I asked my parents, "Why do we have so many girls in the first place?" I always got the same answer: "Because the baby store was all out of boys." But as you'll see in this story, my sisters are actually pretty great. And when you live on a farm, you need all of the help you can get.

My family grew maize, which is another word for white corn. In our language, we lovingly referred to it as *chimanga*. And growing *chimanga* required all hands. Every planting season, my sisters and I would wake up before dawn to hoe the weeds, dig our careful rows, then push the seeds gently into the soft soil. When it came time to harvest, we were busy again.

Most families in Malawi are farmers. We live our entire lives out in the countryside, far away from cities, where we can tend our fields and raise our animals. Where we live, there are no computers or video games, very few televisions, and for most of my life, we didn't have electricity—just oil lamps that spewed smoke and coated our lungs with soot.

Farmers here have always been poor, and not many can afford an education. Seeing a doctor is also difficult, since most of us don't own cars. From the time we're born, we're given a life with very few options. Because of this poverty and lack of knowledge, Malawians found help wherever we could.

Many of us turned to magic—which is how my story begins.

You see, before I discovered the miracles of science, I believed that magic ruled the world. Not magician magic, like pulling rabbits out of hats or sawing ladies in half, the sort of thing you see on television. It was an invisible kind of magic, one that surrounded us like the air we breathe.

In Malawi, magic came in many forms—the most common being the witch doctor whom we called *sing'anga*. The wizards were mysterious people. Some appeared in public, usually in the market on Sundays, sitting on blankets spread with bones, spices, and powders that claimed to cure everything from dandruff to cancer. Poor people walked many miles to visit these men, since they didn't have money for real doctors. This led to problems, especially if a person was truly sick.

Take diarrhea, for example. Diarrhea is a common ailment in the countryside that comes from drinking dirty water, and if left untreated, it can lead to dehydration. Every year, too many children die from something that's easily cured by a regimen of fluids and simple antibiotics. But without money or faith in modern medicine, the villager takes his chances with the *sing'anga*'s crude diagnosis:

"Oh, I know what's wrong," the wizard says. "You have a snail."

"A snail?"

"I'm almost positive. We must remove it at once!"

The wizard goes into his bag of roots, powders, and bones, and pulls out a lightbulb.

"Lift up your shirt," he says.

Without plugging the bulb into anything, he moves it slowly across the person's stomach, as if to illuminate something only he can detect.

"There it is! Can you see the snail moving?"

"Oh yes, I think I can see it. Yes, there it is!"

The wizard returns to his bag for some magic potion, which he splashes across the belly.

"All better?" he asks.

"Yes, I think the snail is gone. I don't feel it moving."

"Good. That will be three thousand kwacha."

For a little extra money, the *sing'anga* can cast curses on your enemies—to deliver floods to their fields, hyenas to their chicken house, or terror and tragedy into their homes. This is what happened to me when I was six years old—or at least I thought it did.

I was playing in front of my house when a group of boys walked past carrying a giant sack. They worked for a nearby farmer tending his cows. That morning, as they were moving the herd from one pasture to another,

8

they discovered the sack lying on the road. Looking inside, they saw that it was filled with bubble gum. Can you imagine such a treasure? I can't begin to tell you how much I loved bubble gum!

Now, as they walked past, one of them spotted me playing in a puddle.

"Should we give some to this boy?" he asked.

I didn't move or say a word. A bit of mud dripped from my hair.

"*Eh*, why not," his friend said. "He looks kind of pathetic."

The boy reached into his bag and produced a rainbow of gumballs—one of every color—and dropped them into my hands. By the time the boys disappeared, I'd shoved every one into my mouth. The sweet juices dribbled down my chin and stained my shirt.

Little did I know, but the bubble gum belonged to a local trader, who stopped by our house the next day. He told my father how the bag had dropped from his bicycle as he was leaving the market. By the time he circled back to look for it, the bag was gone. The people in the next village told him about the herd of boys. Now he wanted revenge.

"I've gone to see the *sing'anga*," he told my father. "And whoever ate that bubble gum will be sorry."

Suddenly I was terrified. I'd heard what the *sing'anga* could do to a person. In addition to delivering death and disease, the wizards controlled armies of witches who could kidnap me during the night and shrink me into a worm! I'd even heard about them turning children into stones, leaving them to suffer an eternity in silence.

Already, I could feel the *sing'anga* watching me, plotting his evil. With my heart racing, I ran into the forest behind my house to try to escape, but it was no use. I felt the strange warmth of his magic eye shining through the trees. He had me. At any moment, I would emerge from the forest as a beetle, or a trembling mouse to be eaten by the hawks. Knowing my time was short, I hurried home to where my father was plucking a pile of maize and tumbled into his lap.

"It was me!" I shouted, tears running down my cheeks. "I ate the stolen gum. I don't want to die, Papa. Please don't let them take me."

My father looked at me for a second and shook his head. "It was you, *eh?*" he said, then kind of smiled.

Didn't he realize I was in trouble?

"Well," he said, and his knees popped as he rose from his chair. My father was a big man. "Don't worry, William. I'll find the trader and explain. I'm sure we can work something out."

That afternoon, my father walked five miles to the trader's house and told him what had happened. And even though I'd only eaten a few of the gumballs, he paid the man for the entire bag, which was nearly all the money we possessed. That evening after supper, my life having been saved, I asked my father if he truly believed I was in trouble. He became very serious.

"Oh yes, we were just in time," he said, then started laughing so hard his chair began to squeak. *"William, who knows what was in store for you?"*

My fear of wizards and magic only grew worse whenever Grandpa told stories. If you saw my grandpa, you might think he was a kind of wizard himself. He was so old that he couldn't remember the year he'd been born. So cracked and wrinkled that his hands and feet looked as if they were chiseled from stone. And his clothes! Grandpa insisted on wearing the same tattered coat and trousers every day. Whenever he emerged from the forest, puffing on his hand-rolled cigar, you'd think one of the trees had grown legs and started walking.

It was Grandpa who told me the greatest story about magic I'd ever heard. Long ago, before the giant maize and tobacco farms came along and cleared away our great forests, when a person could lose track of the sun inside the trees, the land was rich with antelope, zebra, and wildebeest—also lions, hippos, and leopards. Grandpa was a famous hunter, so good with his bow and arrow that it became his duty to protect his village and provide its meat.

One day while Grandpa was out hunting, he came across a man who'd been killed by a poisonous pit viper. He alerted the nearest village, and soon after, they returned with their witch doctor.

The *sing'anga* took one look at the dead man, then reached into his bag and tossed some medicines into the trees. Seconds later, the earth began to move as hundreds of vipers slithered out of the shadows and gathered around the corpse, hypnotized by the spell. The wizard then stood on the dead man's chest and drank a cup of potion, which seemed to flow through his feet and into the lifeless body. Then, to Grandpa's amazement, the dead man's fingers began to move and he sat up. Together, he and the wizard inspected the fangs of each snake, looking for the one that had bitten him.

"Believe it," Grandpa told me. "I saw this with my own eyes."

I certainly believed it, along with every other story about witches and things unexplained. Whenever I went down the dark trails alone, my imagination spun wild.

What scared me most were the *Gule Wamkulu*, the magical dancers that lived in the murky shadows of the forest. They sometimes appeared in the daylight, performing in tribal ceremonies when we Chewa boys became men. They were not real people, we were told, but spirits of our dead ancestors sent to roam the earth. Their appearance was ghastly: Each had the face and skin of animals and some walked on stilts to appear taller. Once, I saw one scurry backward up a pole like a spider. And when they danced, it was as if one thousand men were inside their bodies, each moving in the opposite direction.

When the *Gule Wamkulu* weren't performing, they traveled the forests and *dambos* looking for young boys to take back to the graveyards. What happened to you there, I never wanted to know. Whenever I saw one, even at a ceremony, I dropped everything and ran. Once, when I was very young, a magic dancer suddenly appeared in our courtyard. His head was wrapped in a flour sack, but underneath was the long nose of an elephant and a gaping hole for a mouth. My mother and father were in the fields, so my sisters and I ran for the bush, where we watched the dancer snatch our favorite chicken.

Unlike the *Gule Wamkulu* or *sing'anga* in the market, most witches and wizards never revealed their identity. In the places where they practiced their magic, mystery abounded like strange weather. In the nearby town of Ntchisi, men with bald heads, standing as tall as trees, walked the roads at night. Ghost trucks traveled back and forth, approaching fast with their headlights flashing and engines revving loud. Yet when the lights finally passed, there was no truck attached. In one of the neighboring villages, I heard about a man who'd been shrunk so small by a wizard that his wife kept him in a Coke bottle.

In addition to casting spells for curses, the *sing'anga* often battled one another. At night, they piled aboard their planes and prowled the skies, looking for children to kidnap as soldiers. The witch planes could be anything: a wooden bowl, a broom, a simple hat. And each was capable of traveling great distances—Malawi to New York, for example—in a single minute. Children were used as guinea pigs and sent to test the powers of rival wizards. Other nights, they'd visit camps of other witch children for games of mystical soccer, where the balls were human heads stolen from people as they slept.

Lying in bed at night, I would become so frightened thinking about these things that I'd cry out for my father.

"Papa!" I'd shout, summoning him to my door. "I can't sleep. I'm afraid."

My father had no place for magic in his life. To me, this made him seem even stronger. As a devout Presbyterian, he believed that God—not juju—was his best protection.

"Respect the wizards," he would tell me, straightening my bedcovers. "But remember, William, with God on your side, they have no power against you."

I trusted my father, but as I got older, I began to wonder how his explanation accounted for Chuck Norris, Terminator, and Rambo—who arrived at the Wimbe trading center one summer and caused all kinds of ruckus.

These men appeared in action movies that played in the local "video show"—which was really just a mud hut with benches, a television, and a VCR. At night, wonderful and mysterious things happened there, but since I wasn't allowed out after dark, I never saw any of them. Instead, I had to hear stories the next morning from friends whose parents weren't so strict.

"Last night I watched the best of all movies," said my friend Peter. "Rambo jumped from the top of the mountain and was still firing his gun when he landed at the bottom. Everyone in front of him died and the entire mountain exploded." He pretended to clutch a machine gun and fire in all directions.

"When will they start showing these films during the day?" I said. "I never get to see anything."

The night *The Terminator* came to the video show, it was simply shocking. When Peter found me the next morning, he was still in a state.

"William, I just don't understand this movie. This man was shot left, right, and center, and yet he still managed to live. I'm telling you, this Terminator must be the greatest wizard *ever*."

It sounded fantastic. "Do you think the Americans have such magic?" I asked. "I don't believe it."

"This is what I saw," Peter said. "I'm telling you it's true."

Although years would pass before I saw any of these films, they began influencing our games at home. One was a shooting game that I played with my cousin Geoffrey, using toy guns we made from a *mpoloni* bush. Finding a straight branch, we removed its core, like taking out the insides of a ballpoint pen, and used it as a ramrod to fire paper spitballs.

I was the captain of one team, and Geoffrey was the captain of the other. Along with our cousins, we formed squads and hunted one another between the houses in our village.

"You go left, and I'll go right!" I instructed my soldiers one afternoon, then crawled on hands and knees through the red dirt. My poor mother was constantly scrubbing our clothes.

Right away I spotted Geoffrey's trousers from around the corner of the house. Slowly, without spooking the chickens, I snuck up behind for an easy ambush.

"*Tonga!*" I shouted, then jammed the ramrod, sending a shower of slime into his face.

He clutched his heart and fell to the ground. "*Eh, mayo ine!*" he gasped. "You got me."

We were a solid gang of three: me, Geoffrey, and our friend Gilbert. Gilbert's father was the chief of our whole Wimbe district, a man whom everyone called Chief Wimbe, even though his real name was Albert. When Geoffrey and I got bored with playing our games in the courtyard, we often headed to Gilbert's.

"Let's see how many chickens we can count," I said, taking off down the path.

Going over to Gilbert's house was always fun, since the chief's work was never finished. As usual, we found a long line of truck drivers, farmers, traders, and market women, all waiting to voice their concerns. As we suspected, many of them carried a chicken under their arm—a gift for their chief.

"I counted ten," Geoffrey whispered.

"*Yah*," I said. "Must be lots of problems today."

The chief's messenger and bodyguard, Mister Ngwata, stood at the door in his short pants and army boots, dressed as a police officer. It was Mister Ngwata's job to protect the chief and filter all of his visitors. He was also the chicken collector.

"Come, come," he said, and motioned us inside.

The chief sat on the sofa in the living room, dressed in a crisp shirt and nice trousers. Chiefs usually dressed like business people, never in feathers and animal skins. That's in the movies. Another thing about Chief Wimbe was that he loved his cat, which was black and white but had no name. In Malawi, only dogs are given names, I don't know why.

We found Gilbert in his room singing to the radio.

Gilbert had the most beautiful voice and dreamed of becoming a famous singer. My voice sounded like one of the guinea fowl that screeched in our trees as it pooped, but I never let that stop me from singing.

"Gilbert, *bo*!"

"*Bo*!"

"Sharp?"

"Sharp!"

That was our slang we used every time we saw one another. The word *bo* was short for *bonjour*, started by some chaps who were learning French in school and wanting to show off. (It means hello in that language.) I don't know where *sharp* came from, but it was like saying, "Are you cool?" If we were feeling really good, we went a bit further:

"Sure?"

"Sure!"

"Fit?"

"Fit!"

"*Ehhhh*."

"Let's go to the trading center," I said. "I bet there's a mountain of treasure outside Ofesi."

Ofesi Boozing Centre was the local bar in Wimbe. Its most popular drink was Shake Shake, a kind of beer made from corn that was sold in cardboard cartons. I wasn't allowed inside Ofesi, but I'm guessing they didn't have a garbage can, because every night the men tossed their empty cartons into the road. Gilbert, Geoffrey, and I liked to collect them. After we washed the cartons out with water, they made the perfect toy trucks.

Even though we lived in a small village in Africa, we did many of the same things kids do all over the world; we just used different materials. After talking with friends I met in America, I know this is true. Children everywhere have similar ways of playing with one another. And if you look at it this way, the world isn't such a big place.

My friends and I loved trucks. It didn't matter what kind. We loved the four-ton dump trucks that rumbled out of the big farms, kicking up dust. We loved the small pickups that took passengers from Wimbe to Kasungu, the nearest city. We loved them all, and each week, we'd compete to see who could build the best one. I know that in America, you can buy toy trucks already assembled in a store. In Malawi, we built ours from Shake Shake cartons and pieces of wire. To us, they were just as beautiful.

The axles were sections of wire we bought by picking mangoes. And for the wheels, we used bottle caps. Even better were the plastic caps from our mothers' containers of cooking oil, which lasted much longer. And if we took our fathers' razor blades, we could cut designs in the wheels to give each truck its own unique treading. That way, the tracks in the dirt told us if the truck belonged to Kamkwamba Toyota, for instance, or to Gilbert Company LTD.

We also built our own monster wagons, called *chigiriri*, that looked like American go-carts. We made the frames from thick tree branches, careful to find ones with giant knots or a fork that could be used as a seat. We then dug up large tuber roots called *kaumbu* that looked like mutant sweet potatoes, and shaped them into wheels. The axles were poles carved from a blue-gum tree.

After everything was assembled, we tied it all together with vines and hoped it didn't fall apart. To make the car move, one person pulled with a long rope while the driver steered with his feet. With two cars side by side, we held derbies through the trading center.

"Let's race!"

"For sure!"

"Last one to reach the barber shop will go blind!"

"GO!"

After the race, if we had some money in our pockets,

we'd stop by Mister Banda's shop for a cold bottle of Fanta and some Dandy Sweets. Mister Banda ran the Malawian version of a convenience store. On his shelves were packages of margarine and powdered milk, since most people didn't have refrigerators at home to keep milk cold. He also sold aspirin, cough drops, lotions, bars of Lifebuoy soap, and on the very bottom shelf—Drew's liver salts. I have no idea what liver salts were used for, but I'm certain they tasted rotten.

Whenever we entered, Mister Banda greeted us in our usual Malawian custom.

"*Muli bwanji,*" he said. How are you?

"*Ndiri bwino. Kaya inu,*" we answered. I'm fine. How 'bout you?

"*Ndiri bwino. Zikomo.*" I'm fine. Thanks for asking.

After that, it was more of the same stuff:

"You boys keeping out of trouble?"

"*Yah.*"

"Helping your mother and father at home?"

"*Yah.*"

"Well, give them my greetings."

"For sure."

If we were really hungry, we combined our money and headed to the *kanyenya* stand, which was like a Malawian

22

fast-food restaurant. It was really just a vat of boiling grease over a fire, but the fried goat meat and potatoes they served were heavenly.

The man tending the fire would grunt and say, "How much?" and we would answer "Five kwacha" or however much money we had. Five kwacha was less than one American dollar. The man then turned around and cut a few chunks of meat from a goat hanging from a rail. He dropped the meat into the boiling oil, followed by a handful of sliced potatoes. When everything floated to the top, he served it on a wooden counter, along with a pile of salt for dipping.

"Your mother is a good cook," Gilbert told me once. "But not as good as this."

"*Yah.*"

My parents wanted me home before dark, but that was my favorite time of day anyway. It was when my father and Uncle John—Geoffrey's father—finished their work in the maize fields and came home for supper. In the kitchen, my older sister Annie helped my mother prepare the food. Since we had no electricity, we still cooked everything over a fire. As Annie fed sticks into the flames, my mother stirred a pot of something delicious, letting the smells escape into the courtyard. Since I was a growing boy, it was hard for me to wait—even if I'd just eaten *kanyenya* in the trading center. With my stomach growling, I'd stand in the doorway begging.

"Just a few more minutes," my mother would say. "By the time you wash your hands and face, it will be ready."

Usually before supper, my cousins gathered in the courtyard and played soccer. Since we had no money for a real ball, we made our own using plastic shopping bags (that we called *jumbos*) wadded together and tied with rope. They didn't have the same kind of bounce as a real soccer ball, but they still allowed us to play. All across Africa, children use the same *jumbo* balls.

If it was the rainy season, when the mangoes were ripe, we filled our pails from the neighbors' trees and ate them for dessert. We bit into the juicy fruit and let the sweet syrup run down our fingers. If there wasn't any moonlight for playing soccer, my father gathered all the children— cousins and all—in the living room, lit a kerosene lamp, and told us folktales.

"Be still and hush up," he would say. "Now, have I told you the story about the leopard and the lion?"

"Tell it again, Papa!"

Sometimes my father forgot the stories and made up

new ones as he went along, creating new characters and outrageous endings. And while we loved hearing these tales, the truth was that real life was sometimes difficult to distinguish from fantasy.

During the times of year when we planted and harvested our maize, two jobs that required lots of work, my father and Uncle John hired someone to help them. The most famous of these workers was Mister Phiri, a man of incredible power. In fact, whenever John and my father needed to clear a new field for planting, they didn't even bother with tractors. Instead they sent Phiri, who yanked entire trees out of the ground as if they were weeds.

Everyone knew that Phiri's secret was *mangolomera*, a kind of magic that delivered superhuman strength. Only the strongest wizards in Malawi could give you this potion, which came in a paste made from the bones of leopards and lions. To get the strength, the wizard cut your skin with special razor blades and rubbed the medicine into your blood. Once part of you, it never left. In fact, the magic only became stronger with time. Only the toughest men like Phiri could live with it inside them.

Phiri was so strong that no person or animal could beat him. Once while working in the fields, a deadly black mamba slithered over his foot and prepared to strike. But

Phiri wasn't afraid. He reached down and whipped the mamba with a blade of grass, leaving it paralyzed. Then he grabbed it by the head and tossed it all the way to Mozambique. People said he carried another mamba in his pocket for good luck, and that snake was too afraid to bite him.

By the time I was eight or nine years old, the thought of *mangolomera* seemed more and more attractive. You see, I was very small, and this led to constant trouble with bullies at school. The worst was named Limbikani, who was tall and muscular and had older brothers at home, which made him even more ruthless.

For some reason, Limbikani liked to pick on me and Gilbert. One day on our way to school, he waited for us on the road and jumped out from a grove of trees.

"Oh look, it's William and his friend Little Chief Wimbe."

"Leave us alone," I shouted, but my voice cracked and gave me away.

Limbikani put his chest in Gilbert's face.

"Where's the big chief, monkey boy? Looks like he's not here to protect you."

He grabbed the backs of our shirts and dangled us in the air like two sad puppies. Then he stole our lunch. This happened again and again.

Not only did my size leave me defenseless against bullies, it also haunted me on the soccer field. I loved soccer more than anything, and each week I'd glue myself to Radio One for Malawi Super League action. My favorite team was the Nomads, whose star player was Bob "The Savior" Mpinganjira. The Savior got his nickname one Christmas Eve when he saved us from defeat against Big Bullets, and I can't tell you how much I hated Big Bullets.

Despite my size, I longed to be a player as worthy as my heroes. Whenever all of us boys gathered for practice and drills, I was some kind of star—in my own mind.

Oh, how I would shine—zigzagging between defenders and firing the ball at missile speed.

Then one day I was displaying my various skills when Geoffrey and some others called out to me, "Hey, Kayira, give us the ball!"

Kayira, as in Peter Kayira.

Despite my love for the Nomads, my greatest hero in all the universe was indeed Peter Kayira—the best player for the Flames, our national team—and to me, a man even greater than the president. To be called Kayira was no small thing. I couldn't stop smiling.

Soon everyone on the practice pitch was calling me

Kayira. Even when I went to the trading center, I was greeted with shouts and praise:

"Hey, Kayira, I heard you play like a lion!"

But when it was time to pick the teams for competition, the captains somehow skipped over me. Thinking this was a serious mistake on their part, I pointed it out, only to be told to sit on the bench. *How could this be?*

Well, I thought, the captains are clever fellows. Perhaps they're saving me from injury, keeping me as a secret weapon for the finals. This made me feel even more special. But while I sat on the sidelines, the other players ran past me and yelled, "Keep the bench warm, Kayira!" or "Kayira, we'll be needing you soon . . . as the *bolela*." A *bolela* was a ball fetcher.

That's when I realized it had all been a joke. I was called Kayira not because of my ferocious skills, but because I was a lousy player. The following summer, I decided to do something about it.

Mister Phiri had a nephew named Shabani who was always bragging about being a real *sing'anga* who possessed *mangolomera*. Gilbert and I suspected he was full of hot air, but we were never sure. Shabani was small like me, yet he boasted like a man three times his size. This made us wonder. Shabani didn't go to school, but worked all day in the fields with his uncle. So he was usually there when I returned home in the afternoons complaining about bullies or sitting on the bench.

One day, after hearing another one of my pathetic stories, he pulled me aside.

"Every day you're moaning about these boys, and I'm tired of hearing it," he said. "I can give you *mangolomera*. You can become the strongest guy in school. All of the bullies will fear you."

Of course, having superpowers was a lifelong dream. On the soccer field, I could fly like a leopard with legs like rocket launchers. *POW!* Reacting to my *mangolomera*, bullies at school would wet their trousers with fright.

My father had always warned me about playing with magic. But now with Shabani standing there, smiling like a mongoose, I couldn't resist.

"Okay," I blurted. "I'll take it."

"We'll do it in the blue-gum forest," he said. "Meet me there in one hour, and bring twenty *tambala*." A *tambala* was like a penny in our Malawian money.

An hour later, I arrived in the forest and waited in the shadows for Shabani, my heart beating fast. Shabani then appeared through the trees, carrying a black bag that contained something heavy.

29

"Are you ready?" he asked.

"*Yah*, I'm ready."

"Then sit down."

We took a seat on the soft red dirt and he opened his bag of wonders. From inside, he pulled out a tiny matchbox.

"In here are the blackened bones of lions and leopards, along with other roots and herbs."

He fished out another package filled with strange dust, which he mixed with the ashes.

"These other materials are extremely rare, found only on the bottom of the ocean."

"So how did you get them?" I asked.

"Look, boy," he snapped. "I'm not some ordinary person. I got them from the bottom of the ocean! I stayed down there for three whole days. If I wanted to, I could turn every person in your stupid village into an ant. So don't play with me, *bambo*. If you want this kind of power, it will cost you lots of money. What I'm giving you is only a small taste."

I didn't even see him pull out his magic razor. Before I knew it, he grabbed my hand and cut into my knuckles.

"Ahh!" I screamed.

"Be still and don't cry," he said. "If you cry it won't work."

"I'm not crying."

My knuckles brightened with blood. For each one, Shabani pinched a little powder and rubbed it into the cuts. The medicine stung like a hundred bees. Once he finished both hands, I exhaled with relief.

"See, I didn't cry," I said, panting. I'd been holding my breath. "Do you think it will work?"

"Oh yeah, it will work."

"When?" I asked. "When will I have my power?"

He thought for a few seconds and said, "Give it three days to work its way through your veins. Once it's complete, you'll feel it."

"Three days."

"*Yah*, and whatever you do, don't eat okra, and stay away from sweet potato leaves."

"I'll remember."

"And lastly," he added, "tell *no one*."

I walked out of the forest rubbing my mangled knuckles. Although they hurt like mad, I had to admit they looked pretty tough. That evening, I hid in my room and spoke to no one.

Three days was a long time to wait, but it worked with

my plan. It was the beginning of the summer holiday, and the following morning I left to visit my grandparents, who lived a few hours away in the town of Dowa. It was the perfect place to receive my powers before coming home a hero.

Well, three days crept by so slowly, I thought I would die from boredom. Worse, my grandmother kept putting me to work cleaning the yard and chicken pens and scrubbing her kitchen floor, which left my arms tired and rubbery. Oh, I wondered, when will I become strong?

But on the fourth day, I awoke and instantly felt different. My arms were heavy, as if laden with stones. I flexed my muscles, and they felt as firm as tree trunks. My hands, squeezed into fists, were as solid as two bricks. Heading outside, I took off running down the dirt road to test my speed. Sure enough, I felt the wind in my face like never before.

That afternoon, my uncle Mada invited me to watch a soccer game at the town field. *Perfect*, I thought. *Here I can test my powers*. Like always, the place was packed with people.

But I had no interest in the game. Instead, I scanned the crowd looking for the biggest boy. When I found him—around my age, standing on the far corner of the field—I walked over and stomped on his bare foot. He let out a cry.

"Excuse me!" he said, hopping up and down. "You just stepped on my toes!"

I stared at him, saying nothing.

"I said you stepped on my toes. It hurt."

"So what?" I said.

"Well, it's rude, don't you think?"

"Then why don't you do something about it?"

He looked confused. "What do you mean?"

"You heard me. Do something, *kape*." A *kape* is a drooling idiot.

"Well, in that case," he said, "I'm going to beat you."

"That's what I was hoping you would say."

We began dancing around in circles and I wasted no time. I unleashed a flurry of punches that were so fast and terrifying that my arms blurred before my eyes. I gave him lefts and rights and a few uppercuts for good measure. My iron fists moved so furiously that I didn't even feel them smashing his face. After a while, though, I began to feel sorry for the guy, so I backed away and took a breath. But to my surprise, the boy was still standing. Worse, he was laughing at me!

Before I could unleash another deadly round, I felt a

terrible pain in my eye, then another and another. Soon I was lying on the ground while his fists pounded my back and stomach. By the time my uncle raced over and rescued me, I was crying and covered with dust.

"What are you doing, William?" he shouted. "You know better than to fight. That boy is twice your size."

I was so embarrassed that I ran back to my grandparents' house and didn't come outside for the rest of the weekend. Once I got home, I found Shabani and confronted him.

"Your magic doesn't work! You promised me power, but I was beaten in Dowa!"

"Of course it works," he said, then thought for a second. "Listen, did you take a bath the day I gave it to you."

"Yes."

"Well, that's why. My medicine doesn't allow you to bathe."

"You never said that."

"Of course I did."

"But . . ."

As you can see, I was clearly cheated. My first and only experience with magic left me with sore hands, a throbbing eye, and a healthy dose of skepticism. Gradually, the witches and wizards didn't seem as frightening or powerful, and I began to look at the world in a different way. I saw it as one explained by fact and reason, rather than mystery and hocus-pocus. But in this world, there still existed the same set of sorrows.

CHAPTER TWO

KHAMBA

In January 1997, when I was nine years old, my family experienced a sudden and tragic loss.

One afternoon, while working the fields, my uncle John became very sick and fainted. My father rushed him to the small clinic in Wimbe, where the doctor diagnosed him with tuberculosis, a deadly disease that seizes the lungs. They advised him to go right away to Kasungu Hospital— an hour's drive. But Uncle John's truck wasn't working. And by the time my father managed to borrow another car, his brother was dead.

It was the first time I experienced someone dying, and the first time I ever saw my parents cry. I especially felt bad for Geoffrey, who was now left without a father. All the following day, people came by his house to comfort his mother and to pay their respects. Every so often, I saw him walk out of his house, crying and looking confused.

"Cousin, what next?" he asked me. "What will happen?"

All I could think to say was, "I don't know."

Following Uncle John's death, things became very difficult. Now that my father's brother and business partner was gone, he had to manage the farm alone. It was now up to me and Geoffrey to help keep the farm successful. We all feared that difficult times were on their way.

Not long after Uncle John's funeral, my uncle Socrates lost his job at a big tobacco estate in Kasungu. The family's home was also there, which meant they were forced to move back to our village. Uncle Socrates had seven daughters, which was great news for my sisters. I myself could not care less about a bunch of girls. But as I helped my uncle unload the moving truck, something leaped out onto the ground.

At my feet stood a big slobbering dog.

"Get back!" Socrates shouted, and shooed the dog away. But it came right back, its eyes looking straight up at me.

"That's our dog, Khamba," he said. "I figured we'd bring

him along to guard the chickens and goats. That's what he did best at the estate."

Khamba was the most unusual thing I'd ever seen. He was all white with large black splotches across his head and body, as if someone had chased him with a bucket of paint. His eyes were brown and his nose was peppered with bright pink dots.

Unlike most other Malawian dogs, Khamba was also big—but still just as skinny. In most other parts of Africa, dogs are used to protect homes and farms. No one buys them as pets like they do in America, and they certainly don't lavish them with rubber toys and fancy food. In Malawi, dogs lived on mice and table scraps. In all my life, I'd never seen a fat dog.

As Khamba sat there watching me, a thick strand of drool hung suspended from his tongue. And he smelled funny, like moldy fruit. As soon as Socrates walked inside, he jumped on his hind legs and planted both paws on my chest.

"*Eh*, get away!" I shouted. I didn't want people thinking I was friends with a dog. "Go chase some chickens or something!"

But Khamba didn't budge. I swore he even smiled at me.

Early the next morning, I tripped over something on

my way to the toilet. It was Khamba, lying square in my doorway, ears perked and waiting.

"I thought I told you to leave me alone," I said, then stopped. I certainly didn't want people to see me *talking* to a dog.

Walking back, I met Socrates in the courtyard. He pointed to the thing now attached to my shadow.

"I see you found a friend," he said. "You know, the good Lord blessed me with seven children, but all of them are girls who don't take much interest in dogs. I think Khamba is happy to have found a pal."

"I'm no friend to a dog," I said.

Socrates laughed. "Sure, sure. Tell that to *him*."

After that, I gave up trying to get rid of Khamba. In fact, I started to enjoy his company. And as much as I hated to admit it, he and I became friends. He slept outside my door each night, and when it got cold, he snuck inside the kitchen and curled up by the pots and pans. And just like Socrates said, he made a good watchdog over our chickens and goats, protecting them from the hyenas and wild dogs that roamed the dark countryside.

Even still, Khamba liked to play games with the baby animals. He chased them around the compound, causing the little goats to bleat and the mama hens to flare their wings and hiss. Whenever this happened, my mother would lean out of the kitchen and pitch one of her shoes at his head.

"Stop that, you crazy dog!" she'd scream, and my sisters and I would laugh. *Look who's talking to animals now!*

Aside from upsetting our livestock, Khamba's favorite thing to do was hunt. By this time, going hunting had replaced most of the childhood games I used to play at home, and Khamba provided the perfect partner. During the dry season, we hunted birds that drank from the *dambo* near my house. And in the rainy months, we followed them into the blue-gum forest, where we set our traps and waited in the thickets. This kind of hunting required patience and quiet. Khamba seemed to understand this naturally, as if he'd been hunting his whole life.

One morning after the rains had stopped, Khamba and I headed to the forest to set our traps. As always, I kept my tools and trap-making materials inside a cloth sack that I tied to the end of my hoe. Inside were a rubber bicycle tube, a broken bicycle spoke, a short piece of wire that I clipped from my mother's clothesline, a handful of maize chaff that we called *gaga*, and four heavy bricks.

I also carried two knives that I crafted myself. The first was made from a thick piece of iron sheeting. After tracing a pattern in the metal, I'd taken a nail and poked holes all around the edges, then popped it out with a wrench. I sharpened the metal into a blade by rubbing it against a flat stone. For my handle, I wrapped the bottom half with plastic *jumbo* bags and melted them over a fire to make them hard. My second knife was a punching tool made from a sharpened nail, also equipped with a handle. I kept them both tucked inside the waistband of my trousers.

We entered the forest just past the graveyard near Geoffrey's house, where the blue gums grew tall. In the distance I could see the small mountain range called the Dowa Highlands that separated us from Lake Malawi, some hundred kilometers away. Dark clouds clung to the tops of the green hills, threatening rain.

"Let's hurry, Khamba. We don't want to get wet."

I found a good spot off the main trail to set our trap, then got to work. The type of trap I used is called a *chikhwapu*. To make it, I first cleared a small section of grass and vines with my hoe until I could see the red dirt. Taking my knife, I cut two thick branches from a blue-gum tree and whittled them to sharp points. Then I pushed them into the soft dirt and made sure they didn't move. I cut the bicycle tube into two strips and tied each piece to the ends of the steel clothesline wire, then tied the rubber strips to the poles. When finished, it resembled a giant slingshot.

The bark from a *kachere* tree is papery and durable and makes a fine rope. I stripped several long sections and tied them together, and made a rope about fifteen feet long. I attached it to the steel wire in my slingshot, then I pulled the rubber as far as it would go, locking it between two bicycle spokes sticking out of the ground. This was my trigger. Once it was set, I stacked the four bricks directly behind the trap and sprinkled some *gaga* on the ground. Whenever birds landed to eat the bait, I'd pull the trigger and release the rubber sling, slamming them into the bricks.

"Let's hunt," I said. Khamba's ears perked at the command and he followed me into the trees.

We hid behind a small bush and waited for our game. About thirty minutes later, a small flock of four birds swooped overhead and spotted the bait. I felt my pulse quicken as they turned and feathered down. I was about to pull the trigger when a fifth bird landed. He was giant, with a fat gray chest and yellow wings.

Come on, I thought. *Just a little more to the right. That's it.*

The fat bird pushed his way into the group and began to feed. With all the birds now inside the trap, I jerked the rope.

WHOO-POP!

The whole flock disappeared into a cloud of feathers and dust.

"Tonga!" I shouted.

Khamba and I raced out to investigate. Four birds lay dead against the bricks, while a fifth managed to fly away. I picked them up and brushed away the dirt, their limp bodies still warm in my hands. I placed them in my pockets.

"Now comes the fun part," I said. Khamba's tail was wagging like mad. "Let's go eat."

Back at the house, I cleaned the birds and sprinkled the meat with a coat of salt. I then sharpened a blue-gum sapling and ran it through the birds like a skewer. In the kitchen, I gathered a handful of sticks and built a small fire. Once my coals glowed red, I held the birds over the embers until each one was sizzling and brown. The delicious smell soon drew my sisters to the door, begging for a taste. My father had to intervene.

"Leave those guys alone. The two hunters worked hard today; now let them enjoy their prize."

The forest birds were small and bony, each one just a mouthful of meat. But even still, they tasted delicious. Khamba didn't worry about bones at all, just swallowed his birds in one quick gulp and wagged his tail for more. I started laughing. "When it comes to hunting, you're very patient," I told him. "But when it's time to eat, that's another story!"

CHAPTER THREE

DISCOVERING A THING
CALLED SCIENCE

The year I turned thirteen, I became aware that things in me were changing—not only my body, but also my interests. I was growing up.

I stopped hunting as much and began hanging out more in the trading center with Geoffrey and Gilbert. We met other boys for endless rounds of *bawo*, a popular mancala game played with marbles on a long wooden board lined with holes. The object is to capture your opponent's front row and stop him from moving.

Bawo requires strategy and quick thinking. I'll admit, I was pretty good and often beat the other boys. This filled me with joy, since several of them had been the ones who'd benched me in soccer.

If I couldn't have magic power, at least I had *bawo*.

Also around this time, Geoffrey and I started taking apart old radios to see what was inside. After a lot of trial and error, we began figuring out how they worked.

Since we didn't have electricity or television, the radio was our only link to the world outside our village. The same was true in many other parts of Africa. In most places you go, whether its deep in the forest or in the city, you'll see people listening to small portable radios. At the time, Malawi had two stations called Radio One and Radio Two, both run by the government. In addition to giving us the news and sports, they also played Malawian reggae music and American rhythm and blues, along with Chichewa gospel choirs and Sunday church sermons.

From the moment I heard sound coming out of a radio as a boy, I wanted to know how it got there. When Geoffrey and I started cracking them open to investigate, it was like spying a secret world.

"Why are these wires different colors?" I asked. "And where do they all go?"

"Hmm," Geoffrey said, "and how do they make it possible to hear Dolly Parton, who lives all the way in America?"

"And how can Dolly Parton be singing on Radio One while Shadreck Wame preaches on Radio Two?"

We had lots of questions. But no one seemed to have any answers, so I set out to find them myself.

After cracking open every radio we could find, Geoffrey and I figured out some things. For instance, we discovered that white noise—that static *shhhhhhhh* sound that you hear between stations—and most other functions originate from the circuit board. This is the biggest piece inside a radio, and it contains all the little wires and bits of plastic. The ones that look like beans are called transistors, and they control the power that moves from the radio into the speakers. I learned this by removing one and hearing the volume greatly reduce.

Before long, people were bringing their broken radios and asking us to fix them. Our "workshop" was in Geoffrey's bedroom, which was piled high with heaps of wires, circuit boards, motors, cracked casings, and countless other pieces we'd collected.

Just like with our toy trucks, we relied heavily on recycled materials and a lot of improvisation. The same applied to the tools we needed to fix radios.

For instance, we didn't have a proper soldering iron to weld the metal pieces to the circuit boards. Instead, I took a thick piece of wire and heated it over the kitchen fire until it was red hot, then quickly used it to fuse the metal joints together.

In order to tell what was broken in the radios, though, we needed a power source. We didn't have any money to buy new batteries, so Geoffrey and I started digging in the waste bins in the trading center, looking for ones that people had discarded.

You're probably wondering, *How can you use a dead battery?* Well, the trick is finding the right kind of dead battery.

Batteries used in handheld radios were deader than dead, mainly because these devices don't require a lot of power and drain the battery of every drop. The trick was to find batteries used in big cassette or CD players. Since they demand such high voltage, the battery would often fail before it was totally empty, leaving a few precious morsels of power.

To test the battery, we would attach a wire to each end—the positive and negative—and connect those to a small flashlight bulb. The brighter the bulb, the stronger the battery. Next, we would crush a Shake Shake carton, making it good and flat, and roll it into a tube. Inside, we stacked the batteries with the negative and positive ends facing the same direction. Then we ran wires from each end of the tube into the radio itself, attaching them to the positive and negative heads where the batteries normally go. Together, this stack of "garbage" was usually enough to power a radio—at least long enough to fix it.

On weekends, Geoffrey and I spent our days in the workshop listening to music while we tinkered. If we were lucky enough to get a cassette player to fix (and if there was enough juice in the batteries), Gilbert would let us borrow tapes by the Black Missionaries—our favorite local reggae band.

"Hey, turn it up!"

"*Yah*. For sure."

When customers came to see us, they sometimes seemed surprised.

"I heard someone here fixes radios," one lady said, looking around.

"Yes," I answered, turning down the music. "That would be me and my colleague, Mister Geoffrey. What's the problem?"

"But you're so young," she said. "How can children be doing this kind of work?"

"You mustn't doubt us, ma'am. Tell us the problem."

"I can't find the stations anymore. There's only static."

"Let me see . . . hmm, yes . . . I think we can manage. You'll have it before supper."

"Make it before six! It's Saturday, and I want to hear my theater dramas."

"Sure, sure."

Often people stopped by to give us compliments. "Look at the little scientists!" one man said. Then: "Keep it up, boys, and one day you'll have a good job."

At this point, I didn't know much about science, or that doing science could be a job. But I was becoming more and more curious about how things worked. For instance, how did petrol make a car's engine work? Why was this foul-smelling liquid so important?

Easy, I thought, *I'll just ask someone with a car.*

In the trading center, I began flagging down truck drivers.

"What makes this truck move?" I asked them. "How does it work?"

But no one could tell me. They'd just smile and shrug their shoulders. Really, how can you drive a truck and not know how it works?

Even my father, who I thought knew *everything*, was stumped: "The petrol burns and releases fire and . . . Well, I'm not really sure."

Compact disc players were just becoming popular in our area, and these things really fascinated me. I'd watch people insert the shiny little wheel, press a button, and suddenly hear music. *How in the world*, I wondered . . .

"How do they put songs on that disc?" I'd ask.

"Who cares?" people would answer.

My neighbors in the trading center seemed happy to enjoy their cars and CD players without explanation, but not me. I was filled with the desire to understand, and the questions never stopped coming. If finding these answers was the job of a scientist, then I wanted to become one.

Of all the things to be curious about, what intrigued me the most were dynamos.

They look like small metal bottles and attach to the wheel of a bicycle. I'd always seen them around Wimbe, but never knew what they did. That is, until my father's friend rode up one evening with a headlamp shining from his handlebars. As soon as he jumped off, the light disappeared.

"Hey, what made the lamp go off?" I asked. I didn't see him flip a switch or anything.

"The dynamo," he said. "I stopped pedaling."

I waited for him to go inside, then jumped on his bike

to investigate. Sure enough, the light came on as soon as I started pedaling around the courtyard. I flipped the bike upside down and traced the wires from the headlamp all the way to the back tire, where the dynamo was attached. It had its own little metal wheel at the top that pressed against the rubber. When the tire spun, so did that wheel. Then there was light.

I couldn't get this out of my head. How did a spinning metal wheel create light? The next time the man came to visit, I flipped the bike over for another look. This time I noticed the wires had come loose from the lamp. While the tire was spinning, I accidentally brushed the bare end of the wire against the metal handlebar and saw a spark.

Aha! My first clue.

I called over my trusted colleague, Mister Geoffrey.

"*Bambo*, bring me one of our radios," I said. "One that works. I'm onto something big!"

"Sure, sure."

Just like with our battery tests, I connected the two wires from the dynamo to the positive and negative heads in the radio—where the batteries normally go.

"Okay, Geoffrey, now start pedaling."

When Geoffrey spun the wheel, nothing happened. So I took the wires out of the radio and re-attached them to the headlamp. When Geoffrey pedaled, the light flickered on.

"Mister Geoffrey, my experiment shows that the dynamo and the bulb are both working properly. So why won't the radio play?"

"Hmm," he said. "Try sticking the wires somewhere else."

He pointed to a little socket in the radio labeled "AC."

"Try here," he said. Lo and behold, when I jammed the wires inside, the radio came to life.

"*Tonga!*" we shouted.

I pedaled the bicycle as Billy Kaunda sang his happy music on Radio Two. Geoffrey became so excited that he started to dance.

"Keep pedaling," he said. "This is one of my favorite songs."

"Hey, but I want to dance too!"

Without realizing it, Geoffrey and I had just discovered something called alternating and direct current. Of course, we wouldn't know its true meaning until much later. But while I was cranking the pedals—so hard that my arm became tired—I kept wondering, *What can do the pedaling for me so that* both *of us can dance?*

Well, the answer was electricity. The dynamo had given

me a small taste of this magical thing, and I soon became determined to try and make some on my own.

Many of you have probably been saying, "But doesn't everyone have electricity?" It's true that most people in Europe and America are lucky to have lights whenever they want them, plus things like air-conditioning and microwave ovens. But in Africa, we're not so lucky. In fact, only about eight percent of Malawians have electricity in their homes, and most of them live in the city.

Not having electricity meant that I couldn't do anything at night. I couldn't read or finish my radio repairs. I couldn't do my homework or study for school. No watching television. It also meant that when I walked outside to the toilet, I couldn't see the big spiders or roaches that liked to play in the latrine at night. I only felt them crunch under my bare feet.

Whenever the sun went down, most people stopped what they were doing, brushed their teeth, and went straight to bed. Not at ten p.m., or even nine o'clock—but seven in the evening! Who goes to bed at seven in the evening? Well, most of Africa.

The only lights we had were lanterns, and not the fancy kind that are powered by batteries. Our lanterns were made from empty powdered milk cans, which we bent closed at the top and filled with kerosene. Our wick was a piece of an old T-shirt, which we ripped into strips and soaked in fuel.

Kerosene looks a lot like gasoline and smells just as bad. Worse, it produced thick black smoke that irritated our eyes and throats and made us cough. And because most people's roofs were made from straw, the lanterns were a real fire hazard. Growing up, I heard many stories of people's homes burning down because someone knocked over a lantern.

Electricity does exist in Malawi, but it's very expensive and hard to get at your house. Getting "on the grid" involves squeezing in the back of a pickup-truck taxi and riding several hours to Lilongwe, the capital city. There you would catch another bus to the offices of Electricity Supply Corporation of Malawi (ESCOM) and wait hours in a stuffy lobby until the sour-faced agent called your name.

"What do you want?" they might ask.

"I would like electricity," you'd tell them.

"Hmm. We'll see what we can do."

After you'd fill out an application and paid a lot of money, they would ask you to draw them a map of your village and house.

"That's me," you say. "I live here."

And if your application got approved, and if the workers were able to find your home, then you'd have to pay more money for them to install a pole and wires. Once you had electricity, you'd be very happy. You'd plug in your radio and dance to the music—that is, until ESCOM cut the power, which they did every week, usually at night. After all of that money and trouble, you'd still find yourself going to bed at seven.

Why does ESCOM turn off the power? Part of the reason is deforestation, which is a real problem in Malawi and other parts of the world. Thanks to the tobacco and maize estates, most of the lush green forests that once covered the country back in Grandpa's youth are gone. The rest is being cut down and used as firewood.

You see, since we don't have electricity, most Malawians (including my family) rely on fires for everything from cooking to heating bath water. The problem is that now the firewood is running low. It's so bad that sometimes my sisters have to walk several miles just to find a handful of wood to cook our breakfast. And if you've ever built a campfire, you know that a handful of wood doesn't last very long.

Without trees and forests covering the land, simple storms can turn into flash floods. Whenever it rains heavily, the water rushes through our farms and carries away the important soil and minerals that help plants to grow. The soil—plus a lot of plastic bags and other garbage—washes into the Shire River, where ESCOM produces all of Malawi's electricity from turbines. The turbines get clogged with mud and garbage and have to be turned off and cleaned—which causes power cuts across the country. And every time ESCOM issues power cuts, they also lose money. This means they must raise prices to get their money back, making the cost of electricity higher and higher. So with no crops because of floods, and no electricity because of clogged rivers and high prices, people continue to cut down trees for firewood. It's like that.

One of the ESCOM power lines was connected to Gilbert's house, probably because his dad was the chief. The first time I went there as a boy, I couldn't believe what I saw. Gilbert walked into the living room, touched the wall, and a light came on. Just by touching the wall! Of course, now I know that he really flipped a light switch. But after that day, I started thinking, *Why can't I touch the wall and get light? Why am I always the one stuck in the dark searching for a match?*

I knew that bringing electricity to my village was going to take more than just a bicycle dynamo, or any wizard's best magic. And anyway, my family couldn't afford to buy either of those things. But I did have one bit of hope. I would soon be taking my final exams to leave primary school. If I passed and advanced to secondary school (what kids in America call middle school), I knew I'd be studying more science. Several schools had special science programs where students got to work on all kinds of experiments. If I could get into one of those places, perhaps my dream of becoming a scientist would come true.

My current school, Wimbe Primary, certainly didn't seem like a place where scientists come from. It was located down the wooded trail from Gilbert's house, just opposite the mosque. It was a community school supported by the government, and the conditions were quite shabby.

The iron sheets on the roof were full of holes, and when it rained, the water poured down on us. The rooms were too small for the large number of students, and some classes were held outside under trees. With all the trucks going past, plus the birds, insects, and people walking around, it was impossible to concentrate. The administrators didn't provide us with lesson books of our own. The teachers always ran out of chalk, and most students never owned a pencil. Ask any child in Malawi to spell their name, or give the sum of two times two, and they'll probably scribble the answer in the dirt with their finger.

Another problem at Wimbe were the toilets—just a few grass huts with a deep hole covered with logs. It didn't take long for the termites to make their nests inside those logs and eat them hollow. One afternoon, they finally collapsed with my classmate Angela squatting atop them. Several hours passed before someone heard her crying from the slimy bottom and helped her out. She was so traumatized that we never saw her again.

In order to graduate from Wimbe Primary and advance to secondary school, I had to pass a test. And it was a hard test. The Standard Eight exam covered every subject and lasted for three whole days.

For several months I stayed awake past dark and studied beside the smoky lamp. I spent hours reading over my lessons in Chichewa, English, math, social studies, and agriculture—a subject that we all had to take because we were farmers. For the most part, my Chichewa lessons were easy, so I spent most of my time working on English, which I found very difficult. For agriculture, they wanted us to know things like how to tell if your animals were sick with infections, and if so, how to help cure them.

Most kids already knew these kinds of things from working with their fathers. But even still, I wanted to make sure my answers were perfect.

I took the test in mid-September. For three torturous days, I bit my nails over equilateral triangles and circumferences, and whether Amprol or iodine was the right kind of medicine for a chicken with blood in its poop. I was a bundle of nerves by the time I finished, but I felt confident. The only bad part was that the grades wouldn't be announced for another three months, leaving me with a lot of time for worry.

Unlike in America, secondary school wasn't free. It cost money to attend, and because of that, most kids in Malawi didn't even bother going. My older sister Annie was already halfway finished with her schooling, and I couldn't wait to have my own chance. Another exciting thing about the upper grades was getting a new uniform. Soon I could ditch the little-boy shorts required for younger students and walk tall in trousers.

Once my exam was over, I waited for Gilbert to finish.

"No more short pants for us," I said when he appeared.

"That's right. And until we start school again, our mornings are free. What shall we do?"

"Let's get Khamba and go hunting," I said. "It's been too long."

"*Yah*. For sure."

We were halfway home when Khamba met us on the trail, tail wagging, as if he'd heard my every word. That afternoon, the three of us hunted for hours until the yellow sun sank behind the highlands. With our sacks full, we walked home under an orange dusk and made a great fire in the courtyard, cooked our birds, and ate like men.

CHAPTER FOUR

THE UNCERTAIN LIFE OF AN AFRICAN FARMER

To me, graduating primary school and being a scientist was loads better than farming, which by then was taking up a lot of my time. As much as I enjoyed my holiday break, most of it was filled by helping my father prepare the maize for harvest.

In Malawi, maize is as important as the water we drink. We eat maize for every meal, mostly in the form of *nsima*, which is a kind of doughy porridge. *Nsima* is made by mixing maize flour and hot water. When it becomes too thick to stir, you scoop it out and form cakes in the shape of hamburger patties.

To eat *nsima*, you tear off a piece and roll it into a ball in your palm, then use it to scoop up your "relish"—stewed spinach, pumpkin leaves, or whatever happens to be in season. If your family is fortunate, maybe you also have some eggs, chicken, or goat meat to go along with it. My favorite meal in the world is *nsima* with dried fish and tomatoes. Yum!

As I said, *nsima* is so important to our diets that whenever we go without it, we feel like a fish out of water. For instance, let's say that someone from America invites a Malawian to dinner and serves plates of juicy steak and mashed potatoes, followed by great slices of chocolate cake for dessert. If there's no *nsima*, the Malawian will probably go home and tell his brothers and sisters, "There was no food there, only steak and mashed potatoes. I hope I can sleep tonight."

Growing a good maize crop is difficult and takes the whole year. It's not just the planting and harvesting that kept us busy, but also preparing the soil, adding fertilizer, and killing the weeds that grew around the plants. Such work required every person in the family. My sisters helped with the planting and harvesting. But mostly they assisted my mother around the house—fetching water and firewood, cooking and cleaning, and helping take care of the little ones, which meant that most of the field work fell on me.

We began in July, when we cleared the remnants of the previous season's harvest. We collected the old maize stalks and placed them into piles. Once they were arranged, Geoffrey and I set them on fire. The best thing about burning stalks were the grasshoppers. The insects liked to burrow in the piles, and once they saw smoke, swarmed out by the hundreds. We caught them and put them into sugar bags.

"How many do you have, Mister Geoffrey?" I'd ask, huffing through the smoky fields.

"Lots," he'd say, holding up his bag. "Maybe fifty."

"*Yah*, same here. Shall we eat?"

"For sure."

The only reason we caught grasshoppers was to roast them over a fire with salt, which we did with great excitement. This might sound disgusting to some people. But trust me, there's nothing more delicious than crunchy, roasted grasshoppers with *nsima*. Of course, Geoffrey and I weren't supposed to be hunting and eating grasshoppers while we worked, but in Malawi, we have a saying: "When you go to see the lake, you also see the hippos."

The hardest work in farming was making ridges. These are the long dirt rows that you see in any field. On my farm, we didn't use a plow or a tractor to dig them, but a hoe. And digging them took all of my time. I'd start in the morning before school, waking up at four a.m. when the land was still dark and cool. My mother would be ready with a steaming bowl of *phala*, which is a kind of oatmeal made from maize. After eating, I'd stumble down the trail dragging my hoe behind me.

"Be careful with that hoe in the dark," my father would call out. "I don't want you cutting off your foot."

"For sure."

The big bright moon threw creepy shadows along the road. I walked quickly, trying not to think about *Gule Wamkulu* watching me from the trees, or the witch planes that flew overhead, looking for fresh recruits. One morning while I was walking, a hyena called out from the bush—*oooooo-we*—and caused me to jump out of my trousers. I've never run so fast.

After digging ridges, we waited for the rainy season so we could plant. The rains usually came the first week in December. My sisters and I moved in a line down the rows. One person made a gash with a hoe, while the other dropped three seeds and covered them with soil and a lot of good wishes. A couple of weeks later when the seed-lings pushed through the ground, we gave each a spoonful of fertilizer to help them grow strong.

Buying seeds and fertilizer cost a lot of money. And because it always happened in December, sometimes it meant there wasn't much left for Christmas. We never had money to buy presents, especially because we had a lot of kids. So for us, the perfect holiday was simply enjoying a luxurious meal of chicken and rice together. If there was any money left over, perhaps we'd get a bottle of Coca-Cola from the market, along with some Dandy Sweets.

Then after December, all the money was gone. Worse, by this time most families' maize supplies were also running low. Outside, it rained night and day. It was a time when people tightened their belts and waited for the harvest, which didn't arrive until May. That's when the maize stalks finally stretched above my father's head, and a whole green field would whisper your fortunes in the wind.

Harvest was like one giant party. Everyone in the family headed into the rows and worked from sunup till sundown, singing, telling jokes, dreaming about the great meals to come.

After we'd spent a week shucking the ears, the maize

was placed in giant bags that went back in the storage room—giving us another year's worth of delicious food. In a good harvest, the bags rose to the ceiling and spilled into the hallway. For poor families like ours, it was like putting a million dollars in the bank.

But that was in a normal year.

In December 2000, everything went terribly wrong. Our first problem was the fertilizer. For years and years, the Malawian government made sure the price of fertilizer and seed was low enough so every family could afford a crop. But our new president, a businessman named Bakili Muluzi, didn't believe the government's job was to help farmers. So that year, the price of fertilizer was so expensive that most families—ours included—couldn't afford to buy it. That meant when the rains came and the seedlings pushed their way through the soil, we had nothing to give them.

"Sorry, guys," I said as I stood in the field. "You're on your own this year."

For those farmers who were able to afford fertilizer, it hardly mattered anyway. Because as soon as the seedlings showed their tiny faces, the country began to flood. Heavy rains fell for days and days, washing away houses and livestock, along with the fertilizer and many of the seedlings themselves. Our district survived without much damage, except that after the rains finally stopped, they never came back. Malawi entered a drought.

With no rain, the sun rose angry in the sky each morning and showed no mercy on the seedlings that had survived. By February, the stalks were wilted and bent toward the ground. By May, half our crop was scorched. The plants that remained were only as high as my father's chest. If you took one of the leaves in your hand, it would crumble to dust. One afternoon, my father and I stood in the field and studied this destruction.

"What will happen to us next year, Papa?" I asked.

He let out a sigh. "I don't know, son. But at least we're not alone. It's happening to everyone."

There was no celebration that harvest. We managed to fill only five bags of maize, which occupied only a corner of the storage room. One night before bed, I saw a kerosene lamp flickering in the hallway and found my father standing in the open door. He was staring at those bags, but not like a man counting his riches. He seemed to be asking them a question. Whatever they told him, we'd find out soon enough.

CHAPTER FIVE
MALAWI BEGINS TO STARVE

Part of the answer arrived in late September. Not long after taking our final exams, Gilbert and I went to the trading center to play a few games of *bawo*. As we walked back to his house, I noticed something odd. About a dozen people were gathered in his yard, talking in low, worried voices. They were mostly women, each wearing brightly colored head scarves like my own mother, and carrying an empty basket.

"Who are these people?" I asked.

"They've run out of food in the far villages," Gilbert said. "These women have come to ask my father for handouts or *ganyu*. Some of them walked for days."

Ganyu was another word for day labor, or a small job such as clearing fields or digging ridges for a little money or food. It's how many farmers in Malawi made a living when times were hard. But I'd never seen this many people at once.

"What's your father going to do?" I said.

"He's going to feed them," Gilbert answered. "He has no choice—he's their chief."

What Gilbert said was true. The drought had destroyed all of the crops in the countryside, and the families in the smaller villages had run out of food. Their storage rooms were empty, and now they were hungry.

I came home and told my father what I'd just witnessed. He'd also seen the lines of women, but didn't seem too concerned. He explained that the government always kept giant stocks of maize for emergencies. In tough times like these, they sold it on the market for a reduced price so that everyone could afford to eat.

"Don't worry," he said. "Whatever the case may be, our family has never gone hungry."

A few days later, however, my father returned from the trading center, where a group of farmers had held a rally. They'd delivered some terrible news: A few dishonest men in the government had sold our emergency maize and taken off with the money.

"They're saying there's nothing left," he told my mother. "This year will be a disaster."

My mother's face seemed stricken. "Only God can help us," she whispered.

After that, hunger came to Malawi.

Due to the shortage of maize, the price doubled in the market. When this happened, people started hunting for food in the forest. One evening before dinner I was feeling a bit hungry, so I walked next door to see if I could snatch a few mangoes from Mister Mwale's trees. When I arrived, he and his family were sitting down to steaming plates of food.

"Just in time," I said.

But when I looked closer, I realized what the Mwales were eating—pumpkin leaves and stewed, green mangoes. They weren't even ripe, and I'm sure they tasted awful.

"You'll find no food here," Mister Mwale said, wrinkling his nose as he chewed.

Later, I saw several men digging ridges in Mwale's field for *ganyu*. They were from the outer villages, and each walked away carrying a handful of those same green mangoes.

A few days later while walking through the trading center, I saw something else I'd never seen. Women had spread out plastic tarps and were selling *gaga*. *Gaga* are the clear-colored outer layers, or chaff, that are removed from the maize kernels in the mill. It's mostly garbage, left on the mill floor and tossed away. Farmers fed it to their chickens and pigs. I liked to use *gaga* in my bird traps. But I'd never seen *people* eat it. Yet here, it was selling in the market for three hundred kwacha a pail—three times what it normally cost. A group of women held metal buckets and crowded around the sellers, pushing one another to get some.

"Move away, I was here first!"

"We're all hungry, sister, there are no firsts in that!"

When I returned an hour later, all the *gaga* was gone. Right then I felt a shock pass through me—as if someone had shaken me awake in the night. I started running home.

Until then, I hadn't worried much about our own situation. Being thirteen years old and always hungry explained some of that. Each meal, I'd stick out my plate and ask for seconds, saying, "That's right, keep it coming!" Sure, I knew about the problems throughout the country, but for some reason, I always assumed they were happening to someone else.

Now as I headed home, I grew more and more afraid.

When I reached the house and opened the door to the storage room, I nearly fainted: Only two bags of grain remained. In my mind, they were already gone.

I started doing the hunger math. Two bags of maize wouldn't last two months. In three months, we'd be starving. Worse, there were still two hundred and ten days—about seven months!—until our next harvest. We hadn't even planted one seed, and once we did plant, there was no guarantee that it would rain, or that we'd even have fertilizer.

A few days later, my father started rounding up our goats to sell in the market. In Malawi, your animals are your most prized possessions, a farmer's only token of wealth and class. Now we were trading them for a few pails of maize.

The men who ran the *kanyenya* stands selling fried meat had enormous power now. The prices they offered for goats, pigs, and cows went lower each day, yet people still lined up to sell.

I noticed one of the goats was Mankhalala, one of my favorites. Unlike the other goats, he loved to play. He'd let me grab his horns and wrestle in the courtyard. He and Khamba had also become friends and would chase each other around the kitchen, irritating my mother.

"Papa, why are you selling our goats?" I asked.

He turned to me. "A week ago the price was five hundred. Now it's four hundred. I'm sorry, William, but if we wait any longer, we'll get nothing."

The goats were tied by the legs with rope and already crying. Khamba heard the commotion and came to investigate. When he saw Mankhalala being led down the trail with the others, he started to bark and jump. Mankhalala then turned around, as if to plead for help. He knew his fate. But as much as it hurt me inside, I had to watch him go. What could I do? My family had to eat.

In early November I started waking up as usual at four a.m. to make my ridges. On the first morning when I walked inside to have my breakfast, my father met me in the darkness.

"No *phala* today," he said.

"Huh?"

"It's time to start cutting back. We need to save our food."

By this time, our supply of maize was just one and a half bags. Breakfast was first to go, and I wondered what would be next. But instead of complaining, I drank a big cup of water, grabbed my hoe, and went to meet Geoffrey in the fields.

I told him about skipping breakfast. "Can you *believe* it?" I asked.

But my cousin simply shrugged. "You're just starting that today?" he said. "I haven't had breakfast in two weeks. I'm getting used to it."

In the early morning, the weather was still cool and I could dig my ridges with great energy. But by seven a.m., my stomach had woken up and realized it was empty. It growled and rumbled and demanded to be filled. Soon the sun was high in the sky and sucking all of my strength. The only thing keeping me awake was my father marching past.

"Make those ridges better!" he shouted.

"But I'm too hungry, Papa."

"Think about next year's harvest, son. Try your best."

It was true: My ridges looked crooked, as if a slithering snake had dug them. Across the field, Geoffrey was hard at work.

"Mister Geoffrey," I called out. "You dig my ridges today, and I'll dig yours tomorrow. Can we make this deal?"

"I'll think about it," he said, gasping for breath, "but it sounds like the same deal as yesterday."

I was trying to raise my cousin's spirits. Ever since his father died, he hadn't been the same. He looked sad, and sometimes he stayed in his room for an entire day and didn't speak to anyone. He was also sickly. At a recent trip to the clinic, the doctor said he had anemia, which is caused by not having a healthy diet. I later discovered that breakfast wasn't the only thing Geoffrey was skipping—food was running low all around.

"I'm joking," I shouted. "But seriously, man, you don't look good. Take a break and get some rest."

"I have no choice," he said, swinging his hoe. "You know my deal."

I also knew that Geoffrey wouldn't be returning to school in the next term. Because of the drought and losing her husband, Geoffrey's mother didn't have the money to pay his school fees. And anyway, she needed Geoffrey and his brother Jeremiah to work and provide food. That day, I pretended not to know.

"Soon your man Kamkwamba will be in secondary school where he belongs," I said, "wearing trousers and walking tall."

"He'll find *us* there," Geoffrey said. "We older boys have plans for Kamkwamba."

"You can't touch him!"

"Oh, you wait and see."

*

Geoffrey wasn't the only one changing. Khamba was also slowing down. I'd always known that his best years were behind him, back when he lived on the estate, but now his age was starting to show. And ever since the drought, he'd grown thinner. The food I was feeding him at night just wasn't enough, I guess. As he got slower, the mice in the fields outwitted him, and other dogs beat him to the scraps in the garbage piles. Khamba no longer chased chickens around the courtyard, but stayed in the shade and slept. I was beginning to see his ribs.

One night when I tossed up a ball of *nsima* for him to eat, he lost sight of it and it landed right on his head.

"What's the problem, old man?" I teased. He leaned over and sucked down the food in one gulp. Some things didn't change.

December arrived with dark skies and heavy rain. All across the region, farmers did their best to plant seed for the next harvest, yet many had abandoned their fields in order to search for food. It wasn't long before their land was choked with weeds.

My father managed to plant a small plot of maize but without any fertilizer. He also found enough seed for a half-acre of tobacco—which would prove a lifesaver in the months to come.

What began as drought and hunger in Malawi soon evolved into full-blown famine. That winter, it would tighten its grip until few people were left standing.

Those looking for food began to cluster in the trading center and along the roads. Groups of men carrying their hoes went house to house asking for work, their clothes soaked from the rain and covered in mud. At each place they heard the same reply: *We have nothing to give*.

While the men searched for *ganyu*, their wives gathered at the chief's house, where Gilbert passed out bags of flour at the door. Already, hundreds of people had received food, and more kept coming. They carried children who cried from empty bellies, and some women were so weak that they fainted once they arrived. After Gilbert's mother nursed them back to health, they continued down the road in search of their next bite.

The famine arrived at our door sooner than I imagined. During the second week of December, my mother milled our last pail of maize, giving us just twelve more meals. As soon as she left, I opened the storage room and peered inside. All that remained were empty bags piled in a corner like dirty laundry. I tried to remember what the room had looked like when it was full, but I just didn't have the energy.

That night, my father called the family into the living room.

"Given our situation," he said, "I've decided it's better if we go down to one meal per day. It's the only way we'll make it."

My sisters and I argued over which meal it would be.

"We should have breakfast," said Aisha, who was twelve.

"I like lunch," shouted Doris.

"No," my father said. "It will be supper. It's easier to keep your mind off hunger during the day. But no person should have to sleep with an empty stomach. We'll eat at night."

My stomach was used to being fed every time it grumbled. Having no breakfast was one thing, but not eating breakfast *or* lunch was a lesson in patience and pain. It was even harder on my younger sisters, who didn't understand why no one would feed them.

"Did you hear me, Mama?" they cried. "I'm hungry!"

"Yes, dear," my mother said. "I heard you. Just try to hold on."

Dinner didn't come soon enough that first night. My

father lit a lantern in the living room and we all gathered around, watching the black soot spiral toward the ceiling. As usual, we started with hand washing. My sister Doris walked around to each person and poured the warm water over their hands while they lathered up with soap and rinsed over the basin. When washing was finished, finally my mother fetched two bowls and lifted the lids.

"Try to make it last," she said, and joined us on the floor.

The first bowl contained *nsima*, but instead of a mountain of steaming cakes, this was one gray blob. It didn't even look edible. In the second bowl, my mother had prepared a small portion of mustard greens. We passed the food around and didn't even bother using plates. The meal was over in minutes.

With less than one pail of flour remaining, I knew that only a miracle could save us, or at least a very good idea. The next morning, my father announced his brilliant plan.

"We're selling all of our food," he said.

It didn't make any sense to me. In fact, it seemed like the worst idea I'd ever heard. But then he explained how we'd use the flour to make cakes to sell in the market. The extra money we earned would go toward buying more food. It was a huge gamble.

That morning, my mother mixed the last of our flour

with some soy powder and sugar and made *zigumu* cakes, which resembled small biscuits. The delicious smell of them baking over the fire drifted through the sheets of rain and onto the road, stopping the *ganyu* men in their tracks. Even the birds became brave and gathered outside the kitchen to sing a woeful tune. The aroma seemed to enter my body like a spirit, slithering into my empty belly and stretching its arms and legs.

Normally when my mother made *zigumu* cakes, she'd let me scrape the bowl with my fingers. In Malawi, this was such a cherished privilege that kids had given it a name—VP, after *vapasi* pot, meaning the bottom of the pot.

"Mama, VP?" we'd ask, our eyes round with anticipation.

But this time was different. My mother used every last drop of batter, as if wiping it clean with a sponge. No VP—only empty pot.

That night, my father made a stand from a broken table and an iron sheet. My mother opened for business the following morning, selling her cakes for three kwacha each. The cakes were heavy and lasted longer in the belly than some of the other cheap breads for sale in the market. If a person didn't have enough money to buy flour, the cakes

81

were their only option. That first day, she sold out in less than twenty minutes.

During these hard times, everyone learned the lesson of supply and demand. The rule of economics says that whenever the supply of something is great (say that farmers have a good crop, like any normal year), the demand will be low and so will the price. But when it's the opposite—when the supply is low, like it was during the famine—the demand is overwhelming and the prices soar into the heavens.

Ever since the country ran out of maize, businessmen had been traveling into neighboring countries like Tanzania and buying it by the truckful. Back in Wimbe market, they raised the price—partly because gasoline was expensive and sometimes the trucks broke down. But also, they charged more because they knew people were starving and would pay anything to stay alive.

Luckily one of the traders, Mister Mangochi, was my father's friend and agreed to cut us a deal. For the money my mother earned selling cakes, Mangochi sold her another pail of maize. My mother took it to the mill, saving half the flour for more cakes, while the other half went to us. It was just enough to provide our blob of *nsima* each night, plus some pumpkin or mustard leaves as relish. It didn't erase our hunger, but knowing our one meal was safe made it seem less painful.

"As long as we can stay in business, we can make it through," my father told us. "Our profit is that we stay alive."

A couple of weeks later, my mother was coming home from the market when a giant truck passed her on the road. Its load was covered with tarps, and some of the other traders said it was maize.

"They're taking it to the government store in Chamama," someone told her. When my mother got home, she called me over and explained the news.

"You will go to Chamama tomorrow. Leave as early as possible."

Chamama was twelve miles away, so of course I grumbled. "Are you sure it was maize and not fertilizer? Because I heard that—"

"Are you listening to me, boy?" my mother snapped. She did not like her children talking back, especially not now. "You go tomorrow."

If my mother was right, it was great news. It meant the government had found surplus maize, perhaps from Tanzania, and would sell it for a discount. With prices climbing higher and higher in the market, it was the only way we could get ahead.

The next morning I awoke at five a.m. and set off on my bicycle for Chamama. An empty flour sack fluttered from my handlebars, and as I rattled down the narrow dirt roads, I noticed many others carrying the same.

"Chamama?" I asked them.

"*Ehhhh*," they replied, nodding.

The government store was located in the central market. When I finally arrived, I saw the lines of people stretched from the door all the way down the road, longer than two soccer fields. One line was for men, while the other was for women and children. Each was getting longer by the minute, so I parked my bike against a fence and took my place among the men.

A cool breeze blew from the lake and kept people in good spirits. But once the scorching sun rose in the sky, the hunger revealed itself in everyone. People suddenly appeared exhausted, as if they hadn't slept in days. The skin around their faces was shrunken and their eyes squinted against the hard light. It had probably been weeks since many had eaten a proper meal, and the government store was their last and only hope of survival. As the sun rose hotter, they grew more and more feeble.

The man in front of me could hardly stay awake. His hands were trembling as if he were cold, and his breathing was heavy and loud. When the line started to move, he couldn't keep his balance and fell down. To my horror, no one helped him up—just simply stepped over him. In the next line, babies cried from hunger and children tugged at their mothers' dresses. If there's one thing I'll remember most about that day in Chamama, it's the sound of crying babies.

After several hours in line, people got restless and angry—angry at the sun and at the people pressed all around whose starvation reeked of soured rags. Angry at the government, at the dust, and at the very air that occupied the emptiness of their stomachs. As we inched closer and closer to the door, their impatience took control. People began to push. Someone shoved me so hard in the back that I grabbed hold of the man in front of me to keep from falling down. A few boys from the end of the line then raced toward the front, squirming into the crowd like mice under a door.

"*Eh*, stop cutting!" people shouted. "We've been here since dawn!"

But they kept coming. Everyone knew that at some point the grain would run out, and no one wanted to be the loser left holding an empty sack. The more people cut in line, the more the others panicked.

Suddenly both lines surged toward the front doors at once. The wave of bodies lifted me off the ground and carried me forward. I felt the air being squeezed out of my lungs and saw the sky disappear above me. I was being swallowed by this enormous, terrifying mob and I was helpless against it.

"Hey stop!" I shouted. "I can't . . . breathe!" But it was no use.

As the mob trapped me in its belly, a strange thing happened. Everything went dark. The screams and moaning of children fell away, the shouting vanished. I drifted in slow motion, as if under water. For a second, I thought that maybe I was already dead, and a small part of me even felt relieved. But no, through the cracks in the crowd, I saw the government building—now closer than ever. The crowd had carried me forward like a cyclone. I managed to plant my feet back on the ground and slither between the bodies. It helped being skinny. A minute later, I reached the front of the pack and stood on the porch of the building. Then I slipped through the doors.

Inside, the office was cool and quiet, and in front of

me was a hill of maize as high as my waist. It was more food than I'd seen in months.

And I'd made it just in time. Outside, the mob had exploded into one giant fistfight. Through the door, I watched a woman fall to the ground and vanish in the dust cloud. Two more women carrying babies on their backs jumped out of the ruckus to avoid being crushed, losing their place in line. They brushed off their clothes and walked away with nothing, and I wondered if they'd make it through another month.

"Hey!" a man shouted. "Next!"

He was shouting at me. "I said *next*!"

I hurried forward and placed my order. I had four hundred kwacha in my pocket, enough to buy the twenty-five kilograms as advertised on the sign outside. But when I told him what I wanted, he informed me there'd been a change.

I could only purchase twenty, but the price remained the same.

"So how much do you want?" he said, not even looking up from his ledger.

"Twenty."

He gave me a ticket and pointed down the line, where several workers used metal pails to scoop the maize. They looked muscular and healthy, nothing like the people outside. The man who measured my maize then cheated me. He threw the bucket onto the scale so quickly that I couldn't see the weight, then emptied it into my bag.

"*Next!*" he screamed.

"But wait," I said, "you didn't even—"

He wheeled around. "If you don't like it, you can leave it here. There are plenty of people behind you. *Next!*"

With little choice, I handed him my money, grabbed my sack, and ran for the door. Despite being robbed, I felt a rush of excitement to be holding so much food, though it quickly turned to fear once I stepped back out into the mob.

A man ran toward me, shouting, "I'll give you five hundred for that!"

Another pushed him aside. "No, boy, I'll give you *six* hundred!"

I pretended not to hear. I strapped the maize to my bike as fast as I could and sped away. Once I reached the road, I didn't stopped pedaling until I saw my family's house.

As I rolled into the courtyard, my mother and sisters greeted me like a hero. I was exhausted, and my clothes were torn and dirty from the crowd. When I tossed the maize onto my father's scale, it confirmed that I'd been shorted.

"Fifteen kilos," I said. "Only half a bag."

My mother told me not to worry. "You did fine. And because of you, we'll eat for another week."

In the days after Chamama, people started selling their possessions to stay alive. One morning during a heavy rain, I sat on the porch and watched a line of them pass like slow-moving ants. Women carried giant pots on their heads containing the items from their kitchen: cups, spoons, knives—everyday utensils of a normal life unhinged. Men lugged chairs and sofas on their backs. One man dragged a heavy dining room table through the mud. They were all headed for the trading center to see how much money or maize they could get. Because what good was a kitchen table when you had no food to eat on it?

Khamba lay sprawled out on the ground at my feet. Every few seconds, his tail flipped in slow motion at the flies that gathered on his back. He was getting thinner and more weak, and I knew it was all my fault.

My mother's one meal per day didn't include our dog. The only way Khamba ate was if I shared my portion, and most days, I was so hungry that I ate it all without thinking. Lately, in the middle of the night, his groans of hunger had roused me from my sleep, and I'd stayed awake burning with guilt. It was difficult to even face him now. So once the rain let up that morning, I left him on the porch and followed the people to the trading center. He didn't try to follow.

The hunger had transformed the town. Most of the shops like Mister Banda's were now shuttered, and the market women had abandoned their stalls. The merchants now joined the multitude of starving people looking for food and selling their lives away.

"*Ndiri ndi malonda*," a man called out. "I've got something to sell. How about this radio? It's yours for a giveaway price."

One man sold the iron sheets from his roof for a cup of flour. A nice straw roof could fetch half a cup.

"What good is a roof when you're dead?" he asked.

A few of the businessmen like Mister Mangochi bought their neighbors' furniture and later gave it back. But the truth was that most people had no money to buy anything. They simply shook their heads and walked away.

Inside the maize mill, a crowd of desperate children gathered around the machine. When the rare woman came to grind a pail of maize, they watched the flour cloud rise from the bucket with dancing eyes. As soon as the customer removed the pail from the spout, the children threw themselves onto the floor and wiped it clean. By mid-December, there was hardly any grain to mill anymore and the building fell to silence.

Then Christmas arrived. Normally, it was my favorite holiday.

In better times, we put on our nicest clothes on Christmas Eve and watched the Nativity play at church. Later that night, my sisters and I would catch swarms of the flying ants that arrived each rainy season, then roast them in a flat pan with salt and eat them with *nsima*. Whereas grasshoppers have a kind of nutty flavor, roasted ants taste like chewy dried onions, except more delicious. When eaten along with beans and pumpkin leaves, they are truly heavenly.

Christmas morning breakfast was typically fresh sliced bread slathered with Blue Band margarine and a mug of steaming Chombe tea. A Blue Band sandwich, washed down with milky, sugary tea, is the greatest combination you can put inside your mouth!

Like anyone, Malawians love meat on Christmas. Early in the afternoon, my father usually kills one of our biggest chickens and gives it to my mother to cook. But Christmas chicken is not served with *nsima*. As I mentioned before—

it comes with rice. Ask any Malawian about Christmas dinner and they'll always mention rice.

But on Christmas 2001, we had none of this stuff. First of all, our chickens had died from disease a few weeks earlier because we couldn't afford the medicine. All that remained was one lonely hen, who became a kind of morose symbol of everything we'd lost. No one dared touch her.

All the churches canceled their Christmas Eve Nativity ceremonies because of the hunger, and that night, my sisters and I felt so weak anyway that we didn't bother catching ants.

When Christmas morning rolled around, there was no sliced bread or Blue Band. No tea. And I knew there wouldn't be any chicken and rice, either. I felt so sad that I sat on the edge of my bed and didn't move. I heard the sounds of the radio coming through my door. The DJ was playing "Silent Night" and it only made me angry. *How dare they play that song?* I thought. I grabbed my hoe and headed straight for the fields—anything to keep my mind off Christmas.

Around noon, my mother did manage to serve us a holiday lunch, but it was just the usual blob of *nsima*. She'd probably worked very hard to save enough flour for that extra meal, but it was impossible to eat with a happy heart.

Afterward I went to see Geoffrey, which made me feel even worse. I found him sitting on his bed, looking thin and tired. Ever since his mother had run out of food the previous month, Geoffrey had been one of the people on the roads searching for *ganyu*. He found work making ridges and pulling weeds, but it didn't provide enough food for his whole family, and often they went entire days without eating. Worse, he'd been neglecting his maize crop.

"*Eh*, man," I said. "I haven't seen you in days. Your field is full of weeds. They're taking over."

"Too busy with *ganyu*," he said. "At first, I went looking for enough food for the month, then the week. Now it's all about tomorrow and today."

I hadn't seen Gilbert in a while, so I walked over to his house. About fifty people were camped out in his yard when I arrived, and the smoke from their fires covered the place in a dismal haze. Gilbert was standing in the doorway.

"Merry Christmas, *eh*?" I said, being sarcastic.

"Not here," he answered.

"Well, surely Chief Wimbe has prepared some delicious chicken and rice?"

Gilbert shook his head in disappointment. "These people have taken almost everything from us. It's only beans and *nsima* today."

My nose caught something terrible on the breeze. It made my lips curl.

"What *is* that?" I asked.

"Oh," he said, pointing toward the campers. "They're not even bothering with the latrine anymore. Now they're just defecating in our grass. Be careful where you walk."

"*Yah*, for sure."

With Geoffrey busy with *ganyu* and Gilbert busy with hungry people, I decided to see if my cousin Charity was around. Charity was a few years older. His parents lived in another village, while he worked the fields around Wimbe. He lived by himself in a kind of cool clubhouse where teenage boys gathered to discuss soccer, girls, and whatever else. I never really knew, since most of the time they kicked me out. Whenever one of them said, "William, I think I hear your mother calling," I knew it was my signal to leave.

This time, though, Charity seemed happy to see me. No one wants to be alone on the holidays. He invited me inside, where a small fire was burning in a cooking pot.

"It's Christmas and I'm starving," he said. "I haven't eaten a thing."

"*Yah*," I said. "I'm hungry too."

The two of us began thinking of ways to get food. The mangoes were all eaten and gone, and the businessmen in the trading center wouldn't dare give us any flour.

"What about James?" I said.

Our friend James ran a kind of *kanyenya* stand, but instead of selling fried goat meat, he boiled the brains and hooves—something called headcheese. Trust me, it's more delicious than it sounds. In fact, my mouth watered just thinking about it.

"Perhaps James will be generous on Christmas and let us have some," I said, feeling confident.

Charity waved me off. "Don't be stupid."

Then his eyes brightened and he said, "But he does throw away the skins."

"Can you eat that?" I asked, twisting my face.

"I'm thinking why not? What's the difference? It's all meat, right?"

"*Yah*, I guess you're right."

The hunger had screwed up our brains.

On the way to see James, we passed the other *kanyenya* stands. A group of wealthy businessmen stood around eating meat and fried potatoes. They laughed and joked as they devoured the greasy bits, not even stopping to swallow before stuffing their faces again. Nor did they seem to notice the crowd of villagers that gathered round just to watch them eat. To these men, the hunger was invisible.

James's stand was just down the road. He was there, as usual, hunching over his boiling pot. As we got closer, I could see a goat head bobbing inside the roiling water, along with some leg pieces. My stomach howled and I had to turn away.

"*Eh*, James," Charity said. "William and I are making a Christmas drum for the children in the village. We're wondering if you could spare one of your skins."

"That's a good idea," said James. He turned and nodded toward a black mound in the dirt, swarming with flies. "Take that one there. I was going to throw it out anyway."

Charity grabbed the hide and stuffed it into a *jumbo* bag, then handed it to me. It was still warm.

"*Zikomo kwa mbiri*," Charity said. "Thanks a lot. The kids will appreciate you."

"Sure, sure."

We hurried back to Charity's house, wasting no time.

"How are we supposed to prepare this?" I asked, peering inside the bag.

"Easy," said Charity. "We'll just cook it like a pig."

Back inside, I added some twigs to the fire and got it going again. Once it was good and hot, Charity and I held the corners of the hide and stretched it over the flames. The hair sizzled and flared and gave off an awful smell. Once it looked charred enough, we took our knives and scraped it away. We did this again and again until it was properly cleaned.

We cut the skin into strips and threw them into a pot of boiling water, adding a little salt and baking soda.

"What's the soda for?" I asked.

"It's how the women make their beans cook faster," he answered. "I'm thinking it works with skin too."

After three hours, a thick white foam formed on top of the water. Charity took out his knife and fished through the froth, pulling out a steaming piece. It was gray and slimy. He blew on it to cool it down, then popped it into his mouth. His jaws worked and worked trying to chew it up. Finally, he swallowed.

"How was it?" I asked.

"A little tough. But we're out of firewood, so let's eat."

I snagged a long piece of skin with my knife and held it in my fingers. It was sticky, as if covered with scalding glue. I stuffed it into my mouth and breathed in, feeling the rush of heat instantly calm my angry belly. As I chewed, the juices sealed my lips shut.

"Merry Christmas," I managed to say.

"*Yah*, Merry Christmas."

Just then, I heard a clawing at the door and realized it was Khamba. He must have smelled the Christmas meat all the way from home and come running. His bony frame was bent and tired, but his tail was wagging. I was glad to see him.

"Give some to that dog," Charity called out. "It's dog food we're eating anyway."

I bent down and rubbed Khamba's head. "Let's get you something to eat, chap. I'm sure you're starving."

I tossed Khamba a long piece of skin, and to my surprise, he leaped up and snatched it from the air. Just like old times. I went to the pot and pulled out two more giant handfuls. After he'd finished his meal, the life seemed to return to his body.

I lost count of how many pieces I ate myself. But after about half an hour of chewing, Charity and I gave up because our jaws were too tired. As the sun went down that afternoon, the three of us sat around the cold fire, content with the warm feeling of meat in our stomachs. Because that's what Christmas was all about anyway.

CHAPTER SIX
MY SCHOOL ASSIGNMENT

The following week, I was at home listening to the radio when I heard something better than any Christmas gift.

"The National Examinations Board has released the results of this year's Standard Eight exams," the announcer said.

I raced into the kitchen to find my mother. "My scores!" I shouted. "My scores are ready!"

I took off running toward Wimbe Primary, leaping over stones and puddles along the trail, for once forgetting about my hunger. I wondered which secondary school I would be attending, Chayamba or Kasungu. Ever since I'd decided that I wanted to be a scientist, I knew these two schools were the best for me. They had the finest teachers, libraries, and laboratories where a scientist could master his experiments. Of course, I didn't care which one I attended—wherever those chaps needed me, I'd happily go.

A crowd of students was already gathered outside the administration building. I pushed my way toward the front and found the list. The various schools were posted with their respective students slotted below. I quickly found Kasungu and scanned the names. Nothing. Moving toward Chayamba, my finger scrolled over the names Kalambo, Kalimbu . . . then . . . Makalani.

Wait a minute, I thought. *There must be a mistake.*

"Here you are, Kamkwamba," said a boy named Michael, who was one of the best students. "Your name is here—under Kachokolo."

Sure enough, he was right. But Kachokolo Secondary was probably the worst school in the district. Like Wimbe, it was a community school and very poor. No science programs. No laboratories. Just rain through a leaky roof.

How can this be? I wondered.

The I saw the exam scores posted on the next board. Out of five subjects, I'd scored only one B—in

100

Chichewa, which was the easiest. Everything else was marked C and D.

I was going to Kachokolo because my grades stunk.

My heart dropped into my stomach. I imagined the long walk to Kachokolo, about three miles away. It was near a big tobacco farm. A river flowed nearby where Geoffrey, Gilbert, and I sometimes went fishing. The road was usually filled with mud.

Michael slapped me on the shoulder and laughed. "Congratulations. If anything, you'll become a great fisherman."

The only good thing about Kachokolo was that Gilbert was also going. His grades stunk too. In any case, in two weeks, we'd be walking the long, muddy road together.

The new year arrived with steady rains that encouraged our maize to grow. The seedlings had sprouted well without fertilizer and still seemed healthy. By now, their stalks were deep green and reached my father's shins.

The rains made everything come alive. All across the region, the flowers bloomed and the forests and bushes blossomed. Everywhere you went, the land smelled rich and fragrant. It was all a cruel joke, of course, because nothing was ready to eat.

In the trading center, the businessmen raised the price of maize to one thousand kwacha per pail. The hungry people who'd long ago turned to eating *gaga* started getting sick when the traders began mixing it with sawdust. When this was discovered, an angry mob formed around the men.

"I spent all of my money, only to get a bellyful of sawdust?" one shouted.

"My children are at home vomiting!"

"You people are criminals!"

The hungry people could complain all they wanted, but with no money in their pockets, they had no power. Several resorted to crime.

One afternoon my mother arrived as usual with her cakes and set up her stand. Within seconds, a crowd of people descended, shouting and grabbing at her things.

"I'll take two," a woman said.

"Give me three," said another.

In this chaos, my mother didn't notice that others were snatching cakes from her basin and running away. One man grabbed three cakes, but instead of fleeing, he sat down and ate them right there.

"Nine kwacha," my mother demanded.

"I don't have any money," he answered.

That evening when she returned, her hair was wild and her face full of worry. "They took almost everything," she said, and she was right. For supper, there were only crumbs.

As the price of maize continued to rise, my mother bought less and less flour. The number of cakes she sold began to shrink, and so did our nightly blob of *nsima*. First it was seven mouthfuls, then five, four, three . . .

"Every time you put *nsima* in your mouth, add some water," she told us. "That way you trick your stomach."

At supper, we kids were careful about our portions. We wanted to be fair. But my sister Rose, who was seven years old, became greedy. Often she grabbed large handfuls of *nsima* and stuffed them in her mouth before anyone could stop her.

"Hey, slow down!" shouted Doris.

"Maybe you should eat faster," answered Rose.

We were all becoming thin, especially the youngest ones like Rose. My parents never scolded her for taking more than her share, but one night Doris reached her breaking point. When Rose grabbed a big chunk of *nsima*, Doris leaped across the basin and began punching her in the face.

"Mama!" cried Rose.

My mother struggled to pull them apart, then collapsed against the wall.

"Please," she pleaded. "I just don't have the strength."

That night we went to bed hungry again with the smell of food on our fingers—a smell that even the hottest water couldn't wash clean.

The worse things got with the famine, the more I looked forward to school. Somehow being hungry in a classroom full of friends seemed a lot easier than being hungry at home.

As the big day approached, I tried my best to get ready. The first problem I encountered was my uniform. Back when we still had money, my mother had sent me to the used-clothing stalls in the trading center to buy a white shirt.

Well, since my wardrobe only consisted of two shirts in total, I ended up wearing the white one a lot and got it dirty. Then we ran out of soap.

Back when the troubles began, we'd been using a bar of cheap Maluwa lye soap, which the whole family shared for bathing and washing clothes. When it finally ran out, we were too broke to buy another. We could wash our bodies with warm water and *bongowe* bushes, which acted like sponges, but a white shirt wasn't so easy. I tried everything: I boiled it over the fire, let it soak until the water was cool, then scrubbed until my shoulders were sore.

Nothing worked, so I started school with yellow circles around my armpits and a gray ring around the collar. What could I do?

That morning, I met Gilbert on the road so we could walk together.

"Gilbert, *bo*!"

"*Bo!*"

"Sure?"

"Sure!"

"Fit?"

"Fit!"

"My friend, this is the day we've been waiting for!"

"Indeed!"

"We should get ready to be bullied by the older boys."

"*Yah*, I think so. Who do you think will hit us first?"

"That's just it. If an older boy approaches us and he's not too muscular, I say we deal with him *straightaway*."

"Good plan."

"So who should hit him first, me or you?"

"Definitely you."

The three-mile walk to Kachokolo took us over the hills and across the maize fields and past the *dambos* where we hunted as boys. The school sat in a valley surrounded by tobacco farms, where I watched tractors plowing a field and the few lucky men with jobs enjoying a day's work.

Once at school we gathered for the morning assembly. Our principal, Mister W. M. Phiri (no relation to the fighter from my father's tall tales), stood before us, dressed in a brown, threadbare suit. He was an older man with a bald head, except for bushels of gray hair that grew around his ears.

Mister Phiri started by saying how happy he was to see such promising students. And he was right: We were a fine-looking bunch, and all of us were so excited to be continuing our education. In Malawi, secondary school was a privilege and an honor. In fact, I was certain that I was experiencing the greatest moment of my life.

"But like in any institution of learning," he said, "this school has rules that must be followed. Every student should be punctual and dressed in the proper uniform. If not, punishment will be swift."

After assembly was over, I was walking to class when Mr. Phiri tapped me on the shoulder.

"What's your name?" he said.

I spun around and froze. "William Trywell Kamkwamba," I muttered, unable to hide my nerves.

"Well, William, this is *not* the proper uniform."

I threw both hands under my arms to hide the yellow stains. But Mister Phiri was pointing at my feet.

"Sandals are *not* allowed," he said. "We require students to wear *proper* footwear at all times. Please go home and change."

I looked down at my flip-flops, which had seen better days. The rubber connecting the sole was broken on one of the sandals, forcing me to carry a needle and thread in my pocket for emergency repairs.

I didn't have another pair of shoes at home. I had to think fast.

"Mister headmaster, sir," I said. "I would put on proper footwear, but I live in Wimbe and must cross two streams to get here. And because it's the rainy season, my mother doesn't want me ruining my good leather shoes in the mud."

He scrunched his eyebrows and considered this. I prayed it would work.

"Fine," he said. "But once the rains are over, I want to see you in the *proper* footwear."

My parents didn't have money for schoolbooks, either.

In Malawi, the schools didn't provide learning materials like they do in America. Even in better times, most students couldn't afford to buy their own books and had to share. At Wimbe Primary, that meant squeezing your bottoms together in the same seat and hoping your friend didn't read faster than you. Luckily for me, Gilbert always had his own books and allowed me to look on. The two of us even read at the same level.

As I mentioned, the conditions at Wimbe Primary had been terrible. Holes in the roof that let in the rain. No glass in the windows to stop the cold winter wind. Lessons held under trees. And of course, I told you the terrible stories about the latrines.

I was hoping for a better environment at Kachokolo, but no such luck. When Gilbert and I arrived at our new classroom, our teacher, Mister Tembo, instructed us to sit on the floor.

"The government sent no money for desks and chairs," he said, looking embarrassed. "Or anything else, for that matter."

Certainly not for repairs. In the center of the floor was a giant hole, where it looked like a bomb had exploded. The walls were chipped and coming apart. A damp breeze blew through the broken windows. And sure enough, when I looked up at the ceiling, I saw a lot of blue sky.

To my delight, Mister Tembo was a kind, soft-spoken man who was patient about the setbacks. Like most teachers in community schools, he lived in a small house next door with his wife and children. His clothes were old and a bit ragged, and the small vegetable garden behind his house could hardly sustain his family. But unlike the farmers, he received a meager salary that allowed for some extra grain during the hunger. Even still, I'd seen his kids in the yard before school, and their arms and legs were as skinny as mine.

Despite the poor conditions, Mister Tembo wasted no time starting our lessons. Right away we began studying history, covering early civilizations in China, Egypt, and Mesopotamia. We learned about early forms of writing and how these cultures communicated with one another. I'd always had trouble in math, but I loved our discussions about angles and degrees and how to use a ruler to take measurements. I remembered hearing those words from the builders in the trading center.

One afternoon we began our lessons in geography. Mister Tembo pulled out a map of the world and asked us to find the continent of Africa, which was easy.

"Now, can anyone find Malawi?" he asked.

"*Yah*, here it is!"

We ran our fingers lovingly over our country. I couldn't believe how small it was compared to the rest of the world. To think, my whole life and everything in it had taken place on this little strip of earth. On the map, the land was green and the lake appeared like a blue jewel. It was hard to guess that eleven million people lived in that tiny space, and at that very moment, nearly all of us were slowly starving.

That week, I realized I'd been wrong: The hunger was just as painful at school as it was at home. All day my stomach growled and gave my brain no peace and soon it was too difficult to pay attention. At first, my classmates and I were eager to raise our hands and answer one of Mister Tembo's questions. A few of us even competed to be the first one called.

"Kamkwamba here, over here!" I'd shout.

But after two weeks, a silence fell over the room each morning and never lifted. Faces became thinner. And since we had no soap or lotions at home, our skin gradually turned dry and gray, as if dusted in ash. During recess, a few of my friends simply walked off campus to search for food and never returned.

None of this mattered anyway. On the first day of February, W. M. Phiri made the following announcement at assembly:

"The administration is aware of the problems across the country, which we all face. But many of you still haven't paid your school fees for this term. Starting tomorrow, the free period is over."

My worst fear had come true. I knew my father hadn't paid my fees, but who was I kidding? We were eating one meal per day. We couldn't afford to buy a bar of soap, much less pay twelve hundred kwacha for my school. Walking home, I got mad at myself for even getting excited and coming in the first place. I'd allowed myself a glimpse of the dream, and now it was crumbling all around.

"What am I going to do?" I asked Gilbert. "I have no choice but to face the music."

"Don't stress," he said. "Just go home and see what happens."

When I arrived home, I found my father in the fields.

"At school they're saying I should bring my fees tomorrow, twelve hundred kwacha," I said. "So we should pay them. Mister Phiri wasn't joking around."

My father stared at the dirt for a long time, then said, "You know our problems here, son. Right now we have nothing to spare. I'm so sorry."

The next morning I stood by the road and waited for Gilbert. For some reason, I still wore my school uniform, but I wasn't going anyplace. When Gilbert appeared and waved, I let him walk past.

"What's the matter?" he said, turning around. "Aren't you coming to school?"

I wanted to cry. "I'm dropping out. My parents don't have the money."

Gilbert looked upset, which somehow made me feel better. "So sorry, friend. Hopefully they can find it."

"Yes, perhaps," I said. "See you later, Gilbert."

I walked down to Geoffrey's house to give him the news. A few weeks before, he'd gotten lucky when a bolt of lightning knocked down a tree in his yard. He'd chopped it into bundles and sold it as firewood along the road. It was enough to keep his family eating for a while—or at least I thought so.

Geoffrey was getting dressed when I entered his room and the sight of him made me gasp. He'd lost so much weight. His eye sockets were sunken and dark, but the white parts of his eyes seemed to glow. *This is what starving people look like*, I thought. They look like ghosts.

"Why aren't you in school?" he asked. "Didn't you get selected for Kachokolo?"

"No money. Today I dropped."

"Oh," he muttered, then went quiet. "Me and you, we're in the same desperate situation. I hope God has a plan for us."

"*Yah*," I said. "Me too."

In the afternoon, I waited by the road to meet Gilbert as he walked home. When he saw me, he was shaking his head.

"Almost everyone dropped out," he said. "Today we were few."

Out of the seventy students, only twenty remained.

CHAPTER SEVEN
A TIME OF DYING

The following week, the *gaga* finally ran out in the trading center. People began living on pumpkin leaves, and when that was gone, they sifted through the garbage for banana peels and old corncobs. Along our road, they dug up tree roots and ate grass, anything to fill their stomachs.

As starvation set in, their bodies began to change. Some people became so thin, they looked like walking skeletons. Others came down with kwashiorkor, a condition caused by the lack of protein. Instead of shriveling like everyone else, their arms, legs, and bellies swelled with fluid and became fat. It was another of the famine's cruel jokes. The reality was that they were dying.

Every day the starving people stopped by our house and begged my father for help. They saw we had iron sheets on one part of our house and thought we were rich, even though they were fastened by stones. Some of the men said they'd walked thirty miles.

"If you have one biscuit, please, I can work," they begged, their bare feet so swollen, they couldn't wear sandals. "We're now six days without eating. If you have just a small plate of *nsima*?"

"I have nothing," my father insisted, "I'm barely feeding my own family."

"Just give us porridge," they demanded.

"I said no."

A few men were too weak to continue and slept in our yard all night. The ground and wood were too wet for fires. And when the rains came in the darkness, they curled up under our porch and shivered. By morning, they were gone.

A few nights later, we were sitting outside having our meal when a man approached from the road. He was covered in mud and so thin, it was hard to understand how he was even alive. His teeth protruded from his shriveled mouth and his hair was falling out. Without saying hello, he sat down beside us. Then, to my horror, he reached his dirty hand into our bowl and ripped off a giant piece of *nsima*. We sat there in shock, saying nothing as he closed his eyes and chewed. He swallowed deep and satisfyingly, and when the mouthful was safely in his stomach, he turned to my father.

"Do you have more?"

"I'm sorry," my father said.

"Okay then," the man replied, stood up, and walked away.

The crowds continued to pour in from the bush. More than ever, they converged in the trading center like herds of crazed animals driven together by fire. Women with gaunt, ashen faces sat alone, pleading with God. But they did it quietly and without tears. Anguish was expressed mostly in silence since few had the energy to cry.

Some traders still spread their tarps in the mud and sold grain, but the units had become smaller and smaller, and its price was like gold, like buying the universe and stars in one half-kilo. Crowds gathered around, but mostly to stare in stunned amazement, as if watching a dream in heaven. Those with energy used it to scream and beg so their families might live.

"*Bwana*, just a small plate of flour for my child. That's all I need. It's for my child."

"*Eh*, if I start with *you* . . ." the traders answered, then said nothing at all.

The ones with energy edged closer, lunging like a wolf pack whenever a kernel fell to the ground, shoveling gravel and all into their mouths.

Each group told a different story of the dead:

"There was the man who'd spent days looking for food," one man said. "One morning he decided to nap under a tree and never woke up."

"I was cooking," said another, "when a man came and sat down. He said he needed to eat. But before the *nsima* was ready, he too was dead."

Others had gone so many days without eating, the first bellyful of food sent their bodies into fatal shock. One woman stepped over two dead men on the road, still pitifully clutching their hoes. Men whose legs had swollen with kwashiorkor tried to drain their giant blisters with a knife, only to die later from infection.

The people on the roads weren't the only ones wasting away. One night in early February, I sat down to eat my small portion of *nsima* and noticed Khamba standing in the open door. His head hung low and his eyes drooped, and by the lantern light, I could count each rib pressing beneath his skin. The walk across the courtyard had exhausted him.

Like so many others in Wimbe, my dog was starving to death.

His last big meal had been the Christmas goat skin, which had given him strength and even added a little weight. But since then, I'd managed to feed him only five times—just a small handful of *nsima*, and little more. I had nothing to give him tonight.

"Sorry, friend," I said, and felt a lump swell in my throat. "I just can't share."

It didn't take me long to eat. When the food was gone and out of sight, I stepped over Khamba and went to my room. I lay down in bed and fell into a strange, fitful sleep. That night I dreamed that my stomach had taken over my entire body, filling up my arms, legs, and head like a great big balloon. But at some point in the dream, it had popped and left only emptiness. It turned out my stomach had only been filled with air. Now it was shriveled and useless, and howled in anguish. I took deep breaths to try and fill it again, but it was no use. My whole body ached.

I have to eat, I thought.

I lay there listening to the rain on my roof, then gathered the strength to move. I got out of bed and made my way outside. I stopped at the kitchen door and peeked in. Khamba was curled up by the fire, which had long lost its heat.

"Khamba!" I shouted. "Let's go hunting!"

The very word made him shoot upright, as if he'd been shocked. He slapped his tail against the floor and struggled to his feet. It had been a year since I'd said those words to him, and still he was ready. In fact, his tail swung so hard, I thought it would knock him back over.

"Let's get some food, boy."

I had no maize or *gaga* for my trap, so I grabbed a handful of ash from the fire pit and threw it into a sugar bag. We set off down the trail toward the Dowa Highlands, which seemed forever draped in turmoil. We walked slowly to conserve energy and I whistled a happy tune to raise our spirits.

The maize in our fields was growing tall and green and I knew it wouldn't be long until we could eat. Maybe a month, perhaps a bit longer. Soon this darkness would lift. I looked across the sky for birds but saw none.

At the trap site, I fastened the rubber to the poles and set the trigger. I sprinkled the ash along the ground and sighed. It looked pathetic.

"Let's hope these birds are as hungry as we are," I said.

If we could get three birds, perhaps tonight I could sleep better. Perhaps Khamba could gain some strength and hang on for another week. I took the rope and dragged it behind a nearby tree, where the dog and I stretched out and waited. He immediately fell asleep.

Fifteen minutes later, a small flock of birds swooped down and landed beside the trap. Khamba's head shot up, as if he'd seen them in his dreams. As they hopped toward the kill zone, I let my imagination wander. I pictured the warm fire in the courtyard, felt my hands rubbing the salt into the meat, then hanging the pieces over the embers. I heard the sizzle and breathed in the rich aroma.

The sudden pounding of my heart snapped me out of my daydream, just in time to see the birds approach the bait. I was about to pull the rope when they realized it was only ash and flew away in a burst of wings.

I exhaled in defeat. I may have even cried.

That night back at home, Khamba fell into a deep, scary slumber. I had a difficult time waking him, even with some *nsima* and pumpkin leaves I'd saved from dinner.

"Khamba!" I shouted. "Supper!"

He opened his eyes and gave me a slap of his tail. I tossed the food into the air, but he made no effort, and it landed with a thud on the ground. Several minutes passed before he could lift himself to eat. His body quivered when he swallowed.

Two days later, I fed him again. It was only some pumpkin leaves, so I walked over and spooned them into his bowl.

"I wish it was more," I said. "But it's all I can manage."

But as soon as the food hit Khamba's stomach, he vomited it back up. I knew the end was near.

"Just wait one month. We'll be feasting in a month!"

The next morning my cousin Charity stopped by the house. He was with his friend Mizeck, whom I didn't recognize at first. Mizeck had always been a big guy, a real bruiser, but now I could see the skull in his face. When he saw Khamba, his voice got a bit crazy.

"Look at this thing," he said. "This dog's pathetic!"

Khamba was half asleep, unmoved by the flies nesting on his coat. He'd long stopped caring.

"I can't even stand to look at it!" he said.

I tried changing the subject. "So what are you chaps doing today?" I said.

"Going to the trading center, as usual," Charity replied. "Perhaps we'll find some *ganyu*, but I'm not so hopeful."

While Charity and I talked, Mizeck kept his eyes on Khamba, like he was obsessed.

He said, "You need to put this thing out of its misery. Take it behind the house and use a big stone."

I pretended not to hear him.

"He's right, William," Charity said. "Can't you see the dog is suffering? Take him to the *dambo* where the water is high. It will be painless."

"W-wait a minute," I said, stammering. "What are you guys saying?"

"We're saying it's time to be a man," said Mizeck.

I wanted to smash his face. "My dog is fine," I said. "He's going to get better. In just a month we'll be—"

"If you can't do it yourself," Mizeck snapped, "then we'll do it for you."

I looked at Charity, who then lowered his voice. "It's the right thing to do, William. Don't worry, you won't even have to bother. We'll stop by tomorrow and take him. He won't feel a thing."

I struggled to find words, some form of protest. But Mizeck's crazy eyes stole my breath. They were yellow like a bitten hyena.

When Mizeck and Charity finally left, I felt dizzy and weak, as if my legs were made of grass. I sat down beside Khamba and watched him sleep. The flies circled and landed, circled and landed. I must have been there half an hour before he finally opened his eyes and saw me, then gave a slow flip of the tail. The way he looked at me, even in this state, made me remember our days together, how we could talk without even speaking.

I decided then I couldn't let Mizeck and Charity take him. I considered my options until the compound grew dark, then finally had my answer. They were right about Khamba; he was suffering. But they were wrong about me. I could be a man.

The next morning, I was sitting with Khamba when Charity appeared in the courtyard. My pulse quickened. He looked at the dog and started toward us. But before he could say anything, I stood up.

"I'm taking him," I said.

"What?"

"I'm taking him to the forest."

He looked confused. "A stone is very quick," he said. "So is the *dambo*."

"This is what I want."

Charity nodded. "It's the right thing to do. We'll do it together. Today."

That afternoon when Charity returned, we walked to the shady place behind my room where Khamba slept. He hadn't moved since the previous night.

"Khamba!" I said. "Let's go hunting!"

His head perked up.

"I said let's go!"

He staggered to his feet, shook once to loosen the flies, and hobbled toward me. It took us ages to get out of the compound. I had to walk backward in front of him to keep him moving. "Come on, boy. You can do it."

We walked down the road toward the highlands. The sun was sinking in the west and colored the hills in a tangerine glow. The air felt warm and dry; it was the perfect weather for hunting. We entered the blue-gum groves that Khamba knew so well. At one point, Charity turned off the trail, and said, "This way."

Khamba and I followed, struggling through the high grass. The tears were hot in my throat, but I swallowed them down. Charity looked at me.

"Don't be upset," he said. "It's just a dog."

I nodded. "*Yah*. Just a dog."

After several minutes we stopped where the brush was thick and the grass reached our chests. The mountains were visible over the blue gums.

"This is a good place," Charity said. "No one will pass here."

It didn't feel right. Sure enough, turning around, I could

still see the top of my house. "This is too close!" I said.

"This dog can't go any farther."

I looked over at Khamba. He'd collapsed in the tall grass under a *thombozi* tree and was panting heavily.

Without a word, Charity started stripping bark from a *kachere* tree to make a long rope. I turned my back and stared into the forest. When his hands went quiet, I knew it was ready.

"Tie him to the tree," I said.

Charity lashed the rope to the trunk of the *thombozi*, then tied the other end to the dog's leg. Once the knot was fastened, he turned and walked away. When I followed, Khamba raised his head and began to whine. He knew I was leaving him. After a few steps down the trail, I made the enormous mistake of turning to look. His eyes were still on me. Then he laid down his head.

"I did a terrible thing," I said, then walked faster through the trees.

Once we reached the compound, Charity went home and I walked toward my room. Along the way, I passed Khamba's food bowl sitting by the henhouse. I picked it up and hurled it against the ground, shattering it to pieces.

It's just a dog, I thought.

I stayed awake long into the night, knowing that

Khamba was just down the hill. If I screamed his name loud enough, I thought, he could probably hear me.

The next day, I avoided everyone and stayed busy in the fields. But once I got home that afternoon, Socrates was there visiting my father.

"Have you seen Khamba?" he asked. "I can't find him anywhere."

"I haven't seen him," I said.

"Hmm. Well, I hope those wild dogs didn't get him."

"Yeah," I replied. "Me too."

That night I tried to force Khamba out of my mind, but I kept seeing him in the tall grass. The image never stayed long, for I was too hungry to concentrate on anything.

The next morning, Charity found me in my room.

"Let's go see what happened to Khamba," he said.

"What do you mean?"

"Let's go see if he's dead." He carried a hoe in his hand and told me to grab mine. "We'll bring them so people will think we're going to the fields. That way we can bury him."

We set off with our tools, but I was too mixed up for conversation. We turned off the trail and into the bush, where the grass was still wet from the morning dew and soaked my trousers. After a while, I saw a white hump on the ground.

"Look," Charity said. "Is he dead?"

We walked closer. Khamba was in the same position as when we'd left him. His head rested on his front paws, and his eyes were wide open. I gasped, expecting him to move. Then I saw his tongue sticking out. It was dry like paper and covered with ants.

"Khamba is dead," I said.

The rope hadn't budged. There'd been no struggle. A terrible thought seized me: After Khamba watched me go, he'd surrendered his will to live. Which meant that I'd killed him.

While Charity untied the rope, I started digging the hole. A furious energy came over me, and I worked faster than I had in months. When the grave was ready, Charity and I pushed Khamba's body inside, then paused.

"So long, Khamba," I said. "You were a good friend."

We filled the grave with soil and left no marker. We even concealed the freshly dug earth with grass and leaves. When Charity and I returned home, we told no one about what we'd done. It's remained a secret all these years, until now.

CHAPTER EIGHT
TWENTY DAYS

Two weeks after I buried my dog, cholera swept our district.

Doctors said the sickness started in southern Malawi back in November. A farmer visiting a funeral brought it north, where it spread like grassfire. Within days, hundreds of people were sick and twelve had died.

Cholera is a highly contagious infection that causes severe diarrhea. People mostly get it by eating food or drinking water that's been contaminated with feces. Across Africa, it's an unfortunate companion of every rainy season. Many villages have poorly built latrines that flood with the rains and pollute the wells and streams where people drink. Blowflies also spread the bacteria after crawling out of toilets and landing on food.

The diarrhea that results is clear and milky and quickly leads to dehydration. If people aren't treated immediately, they could die.

During the famine, people out looking for food became the unwitting carriers. The cholera struck them on the roads and forced them to become sick in the bush. Rain, flies, and cockroaches then spread the infection onto the banana peels, roots, and corn husks that others picked up to eat.

To combat the cholera, the clinic at the trading center started giving away chlorine to clean our drinking water. For months it tasted like metal. They also advised families to cover the holes of their latrines to keep out the flies. My father made a lid from a piece of iron sheeting, but as soon as it was removed, the fat green blowflies swarmed out like a Biblical plague and smashed into your head and face. It was a lot of work trying to swat them and finish your business at the same time. In those days, any signs of diarrhea near the latrine hole caused alarm.

Each morning, the cholera people walked past our house on their way to the clinic, their eyes cloudy and skin wrinkled from dehydration. I'd watch them until they got close, then run down the trail toward home. But as soon as they passed, the starving people would follow.

Between hunger and cholera, we had many funerals in Wimbe.

At home, Geoffrey's anemia grew worse. His legs became grotesquely swollen with kwashiorkor. If you touched his foot, your finger left a mark in his bubbled skin, as if the foot were made of clay.

"Can you feel it?" I asked one day, touching the blisters. "Does it hurt?"

"I can't feel anything," he said.

He also became dizzy and had trouble walking a straight line. One afternoon I was taking him outside into the sunshine, but he stopped and said, "Wait, come back. I can't see." We stood there until his eyes adjusted to the light before we continued.

For months, his mother had only served him pumpkin leaves. And now, like Khamba, my cousin was starving to death. With little else to do, my mother took half of our flour for the day and gave it to Geoffrey's mother.

"There's enough here for porridge," she told her. "It isn't much, but I can't watch my own family suffer."

We were all losing weight, especially me. The bones were now showing in my chest and shoulders, and the rope belt that I'd made for my pants no longer worked. Now I just pinched two belt loops together and tied them off with a stick, twisting more as I got thinner. My arms and legs looked like blue-gum poles and ached all the time. I had trouble squeezing my hand into a fist.

One afternoon, I was pulling weeds in the field when my heart started racing so fast, I lost my breath and nearly fainted. *What's happening with me?* I thought. Terrified, I bent down slowly until my knees touched the dirt, then stayed there until my pulse returned to normal and I could breathe again.

That same night, I sat in my room with the lantern while the hunger played games with my mind. If I sat still enough, the walls began to spin in slow circles, like a merry-go-round. I followed a centipede up the wall for what seemed like hours. When a mayfly flew close to the lantern, I grabbed it by the wings and asked it, "How are you alive? What are *you* eating?"

One thing was certain: No magic could save us now. Starving was a cruel kind of science.

Even my father, once a giant man, shriveled like a raisin. Sharp bones now replaced brawny muscle. His teeth seemed bigger, his hair was thinner, and for once I noticed the scars on his skin. One afternoon he reported having trouble seeing across the courtyard. The hunger was robbing his vision, just as it had Geoffrey's.

It seemed the thinner my father became, the more he wanted to weigh himself. He kept a maize scale hanging by a rope near the tool shed, and one morning I watched his routine. He walked out and gripped the hook, then hung there like a sack of grain, staring up at the needle. He made a grunting sound and said, "Hmm, five kilos. Mama—"

As always, my mother came and looked, but refused to weigh herself. The children were also forbidden. Like many women during the hunger, she'd started tying her *mpango* tight around her waist like a belt. She said it confused her stomach and tricked her heart from beating so fast, helping her to breathe.

At night, she resorted to mind games to help us children.

"You're losing weight because you're thinking about food," she told us. "Don't you know that causes your body to stress and burn more energy?"

My sisters cried. Aisha said, "But Mama, I don't want to become swollen."

"Then think about positive things," my mother told her. "Do that for me."

The one positive thing we could dwell upon was our

maize crop. Out in our field, the stalks had grown as high as my father's chest. The first ears had begun to form, revealing traces of red silk on their heads, and the leaves and stalks were fading from deep green to yellow. While men withered and died all around us, our plants were coming up fat and strong.

"Twenty days," I predicted to my father.

"I'd say you're right."

If I was indeed correct, then we had twenty days until the green maize was ripe enough to eat, what we lovingly called *dowe*. It's equivalent to the American "corn on the cob" when the kernels are soft and sweet and pop between your teeth. All day and night, I dreamed of *dowe*.

By the beginning of March, the maize stalks had reached my father's head. At this stage, the flowers told you everything. Once the red and yellow silk began to dry and turn brown, you could start checking for *dowe*. I'd go from stalk to stalk, pinching the cob to feel the grain. If the kernels crushed easily under my fingers, it was too early. But if they felt firm, then it was time.

Every morning for a week, Geoffrey and I walked up and down the rows, pointing out ones that were nearly done. Then finally I spotted a cob that appeared ripe and gave it a squeeze. It was firm.

"This one's ready," I said.

"*Yah*," said Geoffrey, pointing to another. "And so is this one . . . and this one . . . and this one!"

"Our long-awaited day has finally arrived. Let's eat!"

Using the last of our energy, we ran through the rows pulling the ripe *dowe* and cradling them in our arms. Soon I had fifteen ears, and Geoffrey had the same. We peeled back the first layer of husks and tied them all together, then draped the chain across our shoulders. The sight of Geoffrey and me running through the courtyard with necklaces of *dowe* nearly caused a riot.

"It's ready?" Aisha asked, her eyes wide and excited.

"Ready."

"THE *DOWE* IS READY!"

In the kitchen I stoked the coals of my mother's fire until they burned red. Soon my sisters were crowded inside the door, fighting for space.

"Relax!" I shouted. "There's plenty of *dowe* for everyone."

I placed several cobs directly on the coals, then flipped them until the peels were crisp and blackened. I burned my fingers pulling one off, then stripped the steaming husks and began to eat. The kernels were meaty and warm and filled with the essence of God. I chewed long and slow. Each time I swallowed, I was returning something that had gone missing long ago.

Looking up, I saw my parents in the doorway.

"I don't think this *dowe* is ready," my father said, snatching one off the fire. He pulled off the silk and took his first bite. Within seconds, the blood of life seemed to rush back into his face. He knew we would live.

"It's ready," he said, and smiled.

That afternoon, we must've eaten thirty ears of maize. As if heaven opened up, the first pumpkins in our field were also ready. My mother boiled them, seeds and all, then served up baskets of the steaming meat. My God, to have a stomach filled with warm food was one of the greatest pleasures in life. Geoffrey and his mother started coming over and enjoying meals of pumpkin and *dowe* with us. Soon the swelling in Geoffrey's legs went away and he was smiling like his old self.

For Geoffrey and me, March was like one big celebration. Each morning before work, we made a fire in the fields and ate a big breakfast of roasted maize and pumpkins. I remembered a parable that Jesus told to the disciples, the one about the sower of seeds. The seeds planted along the road get stepped on and damaged, those planted in rocky soil can't take root, and the ones planted in the thorns get tangled in the barbs. But the seeds planted on fertile soil live and prosper.

"Mister Geoffrey, we're like those seeds planted on fertile soil, not on the roadside, stepped on by everyone walking past."

"No, no, not us."

"That's right. We lived. We survived."

CHAPTER NINE
THE LIBRARY

All across the district, the *dowe* and pumpkins were like a great army marching to save us from certain death. Of course, our lives wouldn't return to normal until the harvest, which was still two months away. And at night, the same blob of *nsima* greeted us at supper. But at least it was the start of something better. In the trading center, people began to smile and talk about the future.

As the district slowly reclaimed its energy, students at Kachokolo returned to school to resume their studies. But since my parents still couldn't afford my fees, I was forced to stay home. Besides some weeding, there was little work to do in the fields until harvest.

I spent a lot of time in the trading center playing *bawo*. Someone also taught me a wonderful game called chess, which I played every day. But these games weren't enough to keep my mind stimulated. I needed a better hobby, something to trick my brain into being happy. Day and night, all I could think about was school. I missed it terribly.

Then I remembered that a small library had opened the previous year in Wimbe Primary. It was started by a group called the Malawi Teacher Training Authority, and all the books were donated by the American government. Perhaps reading would keep my brain from getting mushy.

The library was housed in a small room by the main office. I entered and was greeted by a nice lady who smiled and said, "Come to borrow some books?" This was Ms. Edith Sikelo, who taught English and social studies at Wimbe and acted as the school librarian.

I nodded, then asked, "How do I do it?" It was my first time ever seeing such a thing.

Ms. Sikelo pulled back a curtain to reveal three giant shelves that nearly reached the ceiling, each filled with books. The air smelled sweet and musty, an aroma I'd find comforting from that day forward. She explained the rules of borrowing books, then showed me the many titles available. I expected to find primary readers and other boring Malawian textbooks. But to my surprise, these books came from all over the world, places like America and England, Zimbabwe and Zambia. I saw books on English, history, and science, even novels for leisurely reading.

I spent hours that morning sitting on the floor, flipping through pages and marveling at the pictures. For the first time in my life, I experienced what it felt like to escape without going anywhere. The books from other countries were especially fascinating, but I ended up checking out the same Malawian textbooks my friends were studying at school. It was the end of the semester, and my plan was to get caught up before classes started again.

Back at home, I fashioned a hammock from flour sacks and strung it between two trees. I spent my mornings at the library, and during the warm afternoons, I read in the shade.

Right away, Gilbert offered to help with my independent studies. Each day after school he stopped by and explained the lessons.

"What did you cover in science?" I'd ask.

"Weather patterns."

"Can I get your notes?"

"For sure."

But as much as I loved to read, I found it terribly difficult. For one, my English was bad, and sounding out words took a great deal of time and energy. Plus, some of the material was confusing since I didn't have a teacher to explain things.

"In agriculture," I asked Gilbert, "what do they mean by *weathering?*"

"It's when rain breaks apart the rocks and soil."

"Ah. Got it."

One Saturday, Gilbert met me at the library just to look at books for fun. We couldn't study all the time. The first thing I spotted was the *Malawi Junior Integrated Science* book, used by the older high school students. Inside were lots of diagrams and photos of strange and interesting things: people with rabies and children stricken with kwashiorkor, like so many who'd wandered our country. One picture showed a man in a puffy silver suit.

"What's happening here?" I asked.

"It says he's walking on the moon," Gilbert said.

"Impossible."

Turning the pages, I saw a photo of Nkula Falls on

the Shire River, located in southern Malawi. It's where ESCOM operated the hydro plant I mentioned earlier, and where the country got its electricity. The only information I had was that the river flowed downhill until it reached the plant, then *POOF*, there was power. How and why this worked, I had no clue.

But this book explained everything. It said the water turned a giant wheel at the plant called a turbine, and the turbine produced the electricity.

"Well," I told Gilbert, "this sounds exactly like the bicycle dynamo. It lights the bulb by also turning a wheel."

The photo of Nkula Falls made me think about the *dambo* behind my house. During the rainy season, there was always a waterfall.

"What if I put a dynamo underneath it?" I said. "The falling water could do the spinning and produce electricity! We could listen to the radio whenever we wanted."

The only problem would be running wires all the way to my house, which would cost a fortune. And what would I do the rest of the year, when the marsh was just a soggy swamp?

"I guess I'll have to research this a little more," I said.

Later that day, we came across another fascinating book called *Explaining Physics*. It was also filled with photos and illustrations, mainly from England. To my surprise, it answered many of the questions I'd been asking for a long time—such as how engines burned gasoline in order to move, or how CD players read the music on that shiny disc. (For those of you wondering the same, it uses a laser beam!) I found an entire section on batteries. Another photo demonstrated how brakes on a car worked. I'd always assumed that cars used strips of rubber to stop the wheels, like on a bicycle. This book said otherwise.

"Vacuum brakes?" I said. "Wow, Gilbert, I really need to borrow this book."

But *Explaining Physics* was way more difficult to read than *Integrated Science*. The words and phrases were long and complicated and not always easy to translate. After a while, I devised my own system by reading words in context. For example, if I was interested in a photo or illustration labeled "Figure 10" and I didn't know what it meant, I'd comb through the text until I found where "Figure 10" was mentioned. Then I'd study all of the words and sentences around it, often asking Ms. Sikelo to look them up in a dictionary.

"Can you look up the word *voltage*?" I asked.

"Sure, any others?"

"*Resistor*. Oh, and *diode*."

Slowly, this is how I began learning English, as well as the sciences that would soon capture my imagination.

After a couple of weeks of reading this book, I came across the most amazing chapter—the discussion of magnets. I knew a little about magnets because they're found in radio speakers. I'd busted off a few and taken them to school as toys, moving slivers of metal around through a piece of paper.

The book explained how all magnets have north and south poles. The north pole of one magnet will stick to the south pole of another, while identical poles always resist. You've probably experienced this yourself when playing around with these things. In fact, the earth itself has a liquid iron core that acts like a giant bar magnet in relation to its poles.

Magnets, like the earth, have natural force fields that radiate between the poles. The south end of a bar magnet will always be pulled toward the north pole of the earth. That's how a compass works—the bar magnet inside always pulls north to keep you from getting lost.

The most fascinating section was about electromagnets, which work by applying power to a coil of wire. According to the book, you can make them out of everyday objects such as nails and batteries.

When electricity from a power source—such as a battery—passes through a coil of wire, it creates a magnetic field. This magnetic field can be even greater if the wire is wrapped around a good conductor, like a nail. The more it's wrapped, the stronger the electromagnet. The strength can also be increased by using thicker wire, or by applying more power. The book showed giant electromagnets picking up cars and heavy pieces of metal. But smaller ones, it explained, help power simple motors in things like radios and car alternators.

"Aha!" I said aloud. "They're talking about radios!"

I was sitting in my hammock when I read this piece of information. It had taken me over a month to get this far in the chapter, mainly because of all the strange English words to learn. But now I'd reached the juiciest part: "How do these motors work?"

Well, in a simple electric motor, a coil of wire on a shaft sits inside a casing that's actually a large magnet. I knew this much by taking apart radio motors and unraveling the copper wire—mainly to make toys and stuff. When this coil of wire is connected to a battery (or any power source) and becomes magnetized, it gets all charged up and wants to fight with the larger magnet surrounding it. The push and pull between their opposing poles causes the shaft to spin. You know the fans that we use in the summer to keep cool? The blades are spinning around and around because of this fight going on inside.

During all this fighting and spinning around, these motors produce their own kind of energy called alternating current, or AC. There's a second kind of energy called direct current, or DC, but that's mostly found in batteries.

Direct current flows in one direction, from one end of the battery to the other, while AC changes direction and can be used in more ways. It's also easier to transmit. Because of this, most electronics use AC power. The book gave an example of an AC-generating motor: a bicycle dynamo.

"Aha!" I said again, remembering back when Geoffrey and I were playing with the dynamo and trying to power the radio. It didn't work when we'd attached the wires to the battery terminals, which only use direct current. But when we jammed them into the hole that said "AC," the radio had come to life.

The book went on:

"The movement energy [of the dynamo] is provided by the rider."

Of course, I thought. *That's how spinning motion gener-*

ates power—in a dynamo and in the ESCOM turbines on the river.

I can't tell you how exciting this was for me. Even if the words and phrases sometimes confused me, the drawings were clear in my mind. It was like seeing an entirely new language composed of symbols—those for AC and DC, positive and negative, batteries and switches in a circuit, and various arrows showing the direction of current. Right away, I understood this language clearly, as if my brain had known it all along.

About a month later, school ended for the semester and Gilbert had more time to hang out. One morning we went to the library, but as soon as we arrived, Ms. Sikelo hurried us to leave.

"You boys spend hours in here taking my time," she said. "But today I have an appointment. Just find something quickly."

The reason it always took so long was because the books were in disarray. They weren't shelved alphabetically, or by subject, which meant we had to scan every title to find something we liked. That day as Gilbert and I looked for something good, I remembered an English word that had stumped me in one of my other books.

"Gilbert, what does the word *grapes* mean?"

"Hmmm," he said. "Never heard it before. Let's look it up in the dictionary."

The English-Chichewa dictionaries were kept on the bottom shelf. I'd always used the one on Ms. Sikelo's desk, but given her mood, I didn't dare ask her for it.

I squatted down to grab another dictionary, and when I did, I noticed a book I'd never seen. It was pushed deep into the shelf and slightly hidden.

What's this? I wondered.

Pulling it out, I saw it was a textbook from America called *Using Energy*—and this book has since changed my life.

The cover featured a long row of windmills, though at the time I had no idea what a *windmill* was. All I saw were tall white towers with three blades spinning like a fan.

"Gilbert," I said, calling him over. "Don't these look like the pinwheels that you, me, and Geoffrey used to make?"

We used to find old plastic water bottles in the trading center. We'd cut the sides into blades like a fan, drive a nail through the lid, then hang it on a stick. The wind would spin the blades. A kids' toy.

"*Yah*," he said. "You're right. But these things are giant. What are they for?"

"Let's find out."

"Energy is all around you every day," the book said. "Sometimes energy needs to be converted to another form before it is useful to us. How can we convert forms of energy? Read on and you'll see."

I read on.

"Imagine that hostile forces have invaded your town, and defeat seems certain. If you needed a hero to 'save the day,' it's unlikely you would go to the nearest university and drag a scientist to the battlefront. Yet, according to legend, it was not a general who saved the Greek city of Syracuse when the Roman fleet attacked it in 214 BC."

It explained how Archimedes used his "Death Ray"—which was really a lot of mirrors—to reflect the sun onto the enemy ships until, one by one, they caught fire and sank. That was an example of how you can use the sun to produce energy.

Just like with the sun, windmills could also be used to generate power.

"People throughout Europe and the Middle East used windmills for pumping water and grinding grain," it said. "When many wind machines are grouped together on wind farms, they can generate as much electricity as a power plant."

It all snapped together. I turned to Gilbert to see if he was reading the same stuff.

"If the wind spins the blades of a windmill," I said, "and the dynamo works by turning the pedals, these two things could work together."

I remembered what the book had said about the dynamo: *The movement energy is provided by the rider*.

"Gilbert, the rider is the wind!"

If I could somehow get the wind to spin the blades on a windmill and rotate the magnets in a dynamo, I could create electricity. And if I attached a wire to the dynamo, I could power anything, especially a lightbulb.

All I needed was a windmill and I could have lights.

No more smoky lanterns that left us with sore throats and hacking coughs. With a windmill, I could stay awake and read instead of going to bed at seven with the rest of Malawi.

But most important, a windmill could also pump water.

With most of Malawi still reeling from famine, a water pump could do wonders. At home we had a small, shallow well that my mother used for cleaning. The only way to get that water was by bucket and rope. But if I attached a windmill and pump to that well, I could pipe water into our fields.

My God, I thought. *We could harvest two times per year.*

While the rest of Malawi went hungry during December and January, we'd be picking our second crop of maize. The pump could also allow my mother a year-round garden to grow things like potatoes, mustard greens, and soy beans—both to eat and sell at the market.

I began to get excited. "No more skipping breakfast, Gilbert. No more dropping out of school!"

With a windmill, we'd finally release ourselves from the troubles of darkness and hunger. A windmill meant more than just power. It was freedom.

"Gilbert, I'm going to build a windmill."

I'd never tried anything like it before. But I knew that if someone else could build them in Europe and America, then I could build one in Malawi.

Gilbert smiled. "When do we start?"

"We start today."

In my mind, I could picture the windmill I wanted to build. But before I attempted something so big, I wanted to experiment with a smaller model. I'd still need the same materials: blades, a shaft and rotor, wire, and something like a dynamo or small motor to generate electricity from the moving blades.

My father in our maize field (photo by Bryan Mealer)

*At age 3 with my father
(provided by Kamkwamba family)*

The village of Wimbe, with the trading center on the right (photo by Bryan Mealer)

Grandpa with his handmade bow and arrow (photo by Bryan Mealer)

In the library (photo by Bryan Mealer)

My small radio windmill (photo by Tom Rielly)

A close-up of my big windmill (photo by Tom Rielly)

A close-up of the original tractor fan (photo by Tom Rielly)

Outside Kachokolo school (photo by Bryan Mealer)

Inside Kachokolo school (photo by Bryan Mealer)

Connecting wires to a car battery
(photo by Sangwani Mwafulirwa)

My breaker box
(photo by Bryan Mealer)

My light switch
(photo by Tom Rielly)

A dynamo (photo by Manuel Wächter, courtesy of istock.com)

Journalists visiting my windmill
(photo by Sangwani Mwafulirwa)

Wind Farm, Palm Springs, California, USA
(photo by Sergio Pitamitz, courtesy of Getty Images)

Me on my Dartmouth
College graduation day
(photo by Herb Swanson)

Geoffrey and I had used regular-sized water bottles for our pinwheels, but now I needed something stronger. Back at home, I started looking around and spotted just the thing. It was an empty jar of Bodycare lotion that my sisters used to play cricket. It was plastic and shaped like a tub of margarine, with a screw-top lid. Perfect. Leaving the lid intact, I removed the bottom with a bow saw, then cut the sides into four strips and fanned them out like blades.

I poked a hole through the center of the lid and nailed it to a bamboo pole, which I drove into the ground behind the kitchen. Right away, I realized the blades were too short to catch the wind. I needed to make them longer.

In our village, we took our baths in a tiny hut made from grass that was open at the top. We typically installed plastic PVC pipe under the floors to keep them from flooding. Not long before, my aunt Chrissy's bathhouse had collapsed in a storm, so they built a new one right beside it. The old one was still there, however, and I knew there must be some pipe buried beneath the rubble. After twenty minutes of digging around, I managed to pull it free. I sawed off a long section, then cut it down the middle from top to bottom.

Back in my mother's kitchen, I stoked the fire until the coals were red, then held the pipe aloft over the heat. The plastic began to warp and blacken as it melted. Soon it was soft and easy to bend, like wet banana leaves. Before it could cool down and harden, I laid it on the ground and pressed it flat with an iron sheet. Using the saw, I then carved four blades, each one measuring twenty centimeters in length.

Once again, I didn't have the right kind of tools, so I had to improvise. This time, I needed a drill. Looking around my room, I found a long nail and took it to the kitchen.

First, I drove the tip through a maize cob to create a handle, then placed the nail on the coals. Once it glowed hot, I poked holes in both sets of plastic blades. I used some wire to connect them to the bottle, but I didn't have any pliers to twist it tight. Instead, I used two bicycle spokes.

That's when my mother found me.

"What are you doing messing up my kitchen?" she said. If there was one thing she hated, it was kids messing up her kitchen. "Get these toys out of here."

I tried to explain about the windmill and my plan to generate power, but all she saw were some mangled pieces of plastic and a bamboo stick.

"Even little children play with more sensible things," she said. "Go help your father in the fields."

"But I'm building something."

"Something what?"

"Something for the future."

"I'll tell *you* something about the future!" she said, and scooted me out the door.

It was pointless to try and explain. What I needed now was a bicycle dynamo or motor, and I had no idea where I would find one.

Of course, I knew where I could *buy* one. A shopkeeper named Daud had one for sale at his hardware store in the trading center. I'd seen it on the shelf in the months before the famine, wrapped in plastic, so shiny, and so out of reach. I went back this time and sure enough, it was still there. Daud smiled when I approached, so I tried my charm.

"Fine day, Mister Daud," I said.

"Yes, fine day."

"Your family?"

"Oh fine, fine, thanks for asking."

"Say, how much for that dynamo behind you?"

"Five hundred."

I leaned forward and gave him the sorriest look I could muster.

"Yes, but you see, Mister Daud, I don't have five hundred."

He laughed. "*Eh*, you know how it works. Go find the money and come back. It will be here. And if not, I can always order another."

I could get the money doing *ganyu* work, maybe some odd jobs here and there. In fact, I'd heard that guys were making one hundred kwacha a day unloading trucks at the dry-goods store. If I worked a week, I could make enough money.

I headed right over to the store and was the first one there. *I'll get hired for sure*, I thought. I waited and waited. Morning became afternoon. The sun grew dreadful and I'd forgotten my water. Finally, the owner walked out.

"Why do you keep standing here?" he asked.

"I'm waiting for the trucks."

"They come every day," he said, "except Monday."

Just my luck, it was Monday.

That night at home, I hit upon another idea. The bicycle dynamo was the ideal motor for the larger windmill I wanted to make. But for this test model, I could get by with using a much smaller generator. I knew just where to find it.

I walked over to Geoffrey's house and found him in his room.

"*Eh bambo*, do you remember where we put that International radio and cassette player?"

"*Yah*, it's here someplace. Why?"

"I want to use its motor to generate electricity."

"Electricity?"

"*Yah*, from a windmill."

Every time Gilbert and I had visited the library, Geoffrey said he was too busy working his fields. To be honest, he didn't seem that interested anyway.

"We're headed to the library," we'd say. "Wanna come?"

"Go ahead," he'd answer. "Waste your time."

But now, when I told him my idea of building a windmill that would produce power—and then showing him what I'd built so far—he saw things differently.

"Cool! Where did you get such an idea?"

"The library."

Geoffrey found the International cassette player under his bed and I went to work. My screwdriver, in this case, was really a bicycle spoke that I'd hammered flat against a stone. It wasn't anything pretty, but it worked to remove the screws from the radio's casing to allow me inside.

After a little prying and jiggling, I removed the cassette deck and found the motor. It was half as long as my index finger and shaped like a AAA battery. A short piece of metal stuck out from the top like a stem. Attached was a small copper wheel that spun the magnets inside and gave the radio its energy.

Using some wire, I attached the motor to the windmill. My idea was to have the Bodycare lid turn the copper wheel as it was spinning—like two gears in motion. But when I spun the lid, it just slipped against the copper. I needed some friction to make the gears catch.

"What we need is some rubber," I told Geoffrey.

"*Yah*, but where do we get it?"

"I don't know."

"What about from a pair of shoes?"

"Now you're thinking."

The rubber from our flip-flops was too spongy and not durable enough, otherwise we'd be set—everyone in Malawi wore flip-flops. We needed a special kind of rubber, the kind used to make the flats worn by most women in Wimbe. There was only one problem: A company called Shore Rubber was going through the villages collecting old shoes to recycle and make new ones. They were offering a half kilo of salt for each pair, so of course, most women took the deal. I wondered if it was even possible to find used shoes anymore. But it was worth a try.

All day Geoffrey and I dug through garbage piles all over Masitala and Wimbe looking for these shoes. Finally, after sifting through mounds of peanut shells, banana peels, and old rusty cans, Geoffrey held up a shoe.

One shoe.

"Tonga!"

The black flat had been buried so long it was now gray and filled with crusty muck. It smelled like goat skin.

"Good job, chap!" I said.

Using my knife, I carefully carved an O-shaped piece out of the rubber, small enough to slide over the motor's copper wheel like a cap. This took more than an hour to do, but once I pressed it on, the two gears caught just right.

The next step was to test the motor to see if it produced current.

Geoffrey began spinning the blades by hand, and I took the motor's two wires and touched them to my tongue.

"Feel anything?" he asked.

"*Yah*, tickles."

"Good, then it works."

Now the question was: What should we power using this little windmill? We decided it would be Geoffrey's favorite radio, an old Panasonic that he listened to while he worked in the fields. Geoffrey loved his Billy Kaunda music, and sometimes I'd even sneak up on him in the maize rows and catch him dancing.

I held the windmill while Geoffrey popped off the Panasonic's battery cover and removed the cells. Using my knowledge from the books, I assumed that because the radio operated on batteries, its motor produced DC power, which meant we could connect the wires straight to the radio's positive and negative terminals. Geoffrey pushed the wires inside, then twisted them so they connected to the heads.

"What do we do now?" he asked.

"Now we wait for the wind to turn the blades."

Just as I was saying that, the wind began to blow. My blades started to spin and the wheel began to turn. The radio popped and whistled and suddenly there was *music*!

It was my favorite group, the Black Missionaries, on Radio Two, singing their great song, *"We are chosen . . . just like Moses . . ."*

I jumped so high, I nearly disconnected the wires.

"You hear that?" I screamed. "We did it! It actually works!"

"At last!" Geoffrey said.

"Now I'll go even bigger. Super power!"

The success of my small windmill gave me confidence to attempt an even bigger machine, and I'd already started making a list of materials.

I would still use PVC pipe for blades, though I'd need much longer pieces. The blades would have to attach to a rotor, which needed to be some kind of flat metal disc. Plus I'd need a shaft—or axle—to make it all spin.

The best thing I could think of was the bottom bracket of a bicycle. The bracket—or "gav," as we called it—is what attached the bike's pedals to the crankset and turns the chain to spin the back wheel. But in this case, I'd replace the pedals with blades. When the back wheel spun, I'd have a dynamo attached to generate the power. Basically, I was going to hoist a bicycle into the air like a flag to catch the wind. Just trying to imagine it made me laugh.

But of course, none of this changed the fact that I still had no money to buy materials. So like with the smaller machine, I had to go and find them on my own.

For the next month, I woke up early and went searching for windmill pieces like I was exploring for treasure. The best place I knew was an old tobacco plantation across from Kachokolo school. The abandoned garage and scrap-yard were littered with machine parts and stripped bodies of cars and tractors, all forgotten and left to rust. Gilbert and I used to play around there, but never had much use for the junk.

Now I was returning to the yard with a mission. I set out one morning over the hills and streams, noticing how the land hadn't changed much since the end of the rains. The grass was still high and starting to fade to brown, but the maize in the fields was tall and green. Soon we'd be harvesting and our problems would be over, at least for this year.

At the school, I turned into the plantation and stopped at the entrance to the scrapyard. *Behold!* Now that I had an actual purpose and a plan, I realized just how much treasure lay before me: old water pumps, tractor rims half the size of my body, filters, hoses, old pipes, and plows.

Several stripped car bodies lay bleached by the sun, in addition to two abandoned tractors. They had no tires or engines, just rusted gearboxes in their bellies. Inside the cabs, the glass was busted off the instrument panels, but the steering wheels, clutch, and pedals were still intact. Aside from the sound of the grass swaying in the wind, the scrapyard was silent and I was beautifully alone.

The first afternoon, I discovered a large tractor fan—the perfect design for my rotor. I could bolt the PVC blades directly to the metal blades on the fan. That same day, I found a giant shock absorber, which I banged against an engine block to knock off the casing. Inside was a long piston—the ideal windmill shaft.

I needed some kind of ball bearing to connect the shock absorber and gav to reduce the friction. In order to find the right size, I used a piece of rope as a measuring tape and went around to all the various shafts with bearings attached. After three days I found the right match on an old peanut-grinding machine. I used a rusted coil spring to bang the bearing loose, and found it was in pristine condition.

The only problem with the scrapyard was that it sat directly across from Kachokolo school, where I'd left a bit of my heart. The school was currently empty until students returned in a few short weeks. I could see through the windows. For a brief moment, I imagined myself back at my desk.

"Look out," I said. "Your man Kamkwamba will be there soon."

CHAPTER TEN
HARVEST TIME

The only reason I was hopeful about returning to school was that my father had managed to harvest a small plot of tobacco. He had saved the seeds from the previous year, and back in September, I'd nursed the seedlings down at the *dambo* before transferring them to our fields.

Somehow the plants had survived much of the famine and grown fairly healthy—the leaves light brown in color with traces of red. Several weeks earlier, Geoffrey and I had picked the tobacco and hung it to dry under the bamboo shelters.

In a normal year, a crop that strong would fetch a high

price at the auction in Lilongwe. But now with the hunger, we couldn't be sure of anything. Besides, my father had already started borrowing money and maize in exchange for the tobacco once it was ready, which meant that the minute those leaves were dry, we'd have to start settling our debts.

As the first day of school approached, I was getting indications that things were okay. For one, my father had said nothing to me about staying home due to lack of fees. In fact, one afternoon he even handed me a few kwacha to go buy a notebook and pencils. And my mother had purchased a big bar of Maluwa soap, which allowed me to finally scrub the yellow stains from my school shirt.

The night before the big day, I carefully ironed my clothes and laid them on a chair, right next to my school supplies, so they were ready for the morning. I was so nervous that I stayed awake for hours trying to imagine every detail: what I would eat for breakfast, what I'd look like in my uniform, and how I'd greet Gilbert on the road. I desperately missed my friends and the excitement of a classroom.

When Gilbert appeared from the trees the next morning, I ran to meet him.

"Gilbert, *bo!*"

"Bo!"

"Sharp?"

"Sharp!"

"Fit?"

"Fit! Welcome back, friend, it's good to walk with you again."

"Oh thank you, Gilbert, it's good to be here!"

It was great to be back with my pals, all the jokesters and usual entertainers. I saw many familiar faces. We were all still thin, and that wouldn't change until the harvest. But at least our health was improving.

But just as I'd feared, I was behind in everything: geography, agriculture, math, all the subjects I'd studied in the library. My fellow students were working on graphs and variables and scientific names of animals. I didn't know any of that stuff. I struggled for the first two weeks, copying all the notes I could, while trying to get the hang of classes once again. It had been a long time, and so much had happened.

After ten days, the deadline for paying school fees was approaching and I started getting nervous. Something didn't seem right. My father knew my fees were due, but he hadn't mentioned anything. And fearing the worst, I couldn't bear to bring it up. The closest we got was a short conversation one afternoon in the fields:

"So how is school life?" he asked.

"It's going okay, but I'm so behind. I think with time I'll catch up."

"Well," he said, "just work hard."

Despite him saying that, I couldn't help the sick feeling in my stomach. It was still there the morning Mister Phiri gathered everyone for morning assembly.

"Fees for this term are due Monday," he said. "And those students who didn't pay last term's fees must also pay those without delay."

Hey, wait a minute, I thought. Even though I'd dropped last term, I still had to pay those fees? It didn't seem fair. Together, the two terms equaled over two thousand kwacha. Given what my family had just been through, two thousand kwacha was an impossible amount. I knew my fate was sealed.

But instead of going home to face it directly, I tried going to school for free. I snuck in.

I had to calculate my movements carefully. On Mondays and Fridays, Mister Phiri held assembly inside the same classroom. There he read aloud all the names of students who had already paid their fees, telling them, "Go to class straightaway." The students who were still seated had to show a receipt, or else stand up and leave.

Geoffrey had been humiliated this way two years before, so I was ready. On the first day of roll call, I arrived at school with Gilbert as usual. But as soon as everyone went inside for assembly, I ducked into the toilets to hide. I stayed low and scanned the courtyard through the tiny window. The minute Mister Phiri released everyone, I slipped into the crowd unnoticed.

In class, I sat in the back of the room and kept my head down. I never asked questions, for fear of being noticed. As long as I was silent, I thought, I could listen and still learn. I was certain Mister Tembo was wise to my tricks, remembering that I was booted the previous term for lack of fees. But if he knew, he never called me out.

The whole experience was so stressful that each morning I awoke with the same awful stomachache. Gilbert would meet me on the road and try to make me feel better.

"Good morning, friend. I'm happy to see you're trying your luck again."

"*Yah*," I said. "Let's hope today isn't the end."

"Just stay quiet and don't say anything."

"I guess."

Finally, after two weeks, I was busted.

One morning, Mister Tembo read aloud the names of debtors in class, and that's when I was caught. The second my name was called, I stood up and walked to the door.

"Guys, I paid," I said, trying to be cool. "I just forgot my receipt . . . I'll get it and come right back . . ."

Once outside, I began to cry, then I went home and told my father the news.

"I've been expecting this," he said. "I just didn't know when."

But instead of breaking my heart, my father went to see Mister Tembo and pleaded on my behalf. The tobacco would be ready in a few weeks, and after paying his creditors, my father was hoping against hope there'd be enough left to sell and cover my school.

"I'll have the money soon," he said. "Just please let him stay."

Mister Tembo spoke to some other teachers. They agreed to let me to stay in school for three more weeks, long enough for my father to sell the tobacco.

And those three weeks were fantastic, like winning the jackpot. No more sneaking around, no more butterflies in my stomach. Now I could relax, learn, and participate in class. And when the teacher cracked a joke, I laughed at the top of my voice.

"Oh, that's so funny!" or "Good point! I didn't know *that!*"

The other students gave me strange looks.

"These past weeks he's been posing as the cool, quiet guy," one said. "But look at him now."

At the end of three weeks, the tobacco was finally dried and ready, having turned a light chocolate brown in the sun. Once this happened, the creditors began turning up at our house, looking to be paid.

"I've come for my fifty kilos," one said.

"Given our earlier agreement, do you have my twenty kilos?" asked another.

By the time the last trader left pushing a bicycle laden with our tobacco, all that remained was a sixty-kilogram bushel. My father loaded it into a pickup and drove it to Auction Holdings Limited in Lilongwe, where the buyers only agreed to take fifty. After transport costs and government taxes, my father came home with around two thousand kwacha. It was just enough to pay for my school, but then there'd be nothing left for the rest of the family: no money for my sisters' shoes, no cooking oil, soap, or medicine if someone got sick.

Once again, we were broke.

My father tried negotiating again with Mister Tembo,

but Mister Phiri forbade me to return. He said that his boss, the Minister of Education, was visiting various schools to ensure that students were paying their fees.

"If we're caught, we could lose our jobs." said Mister Tembo.

I was sitting in the courtyard when my father returned with the news.

"I've done my best," he said, "but the famine took everything."

He kneeled down to face me. "Please understand me, son. *Pepani, kwa mbiri*. I'm very sorry. Your father tried."

It was too difficult to look at him. "*Chabwino*," I said. "I understand."

At least with daughters, a Malawian father can hope they'll marry a husband who can provide a home and food and help them continue their schooling. But with a boy, it was different. My education meant everything to my father. That night he told my mother he'd failed his only son.

"Today I let down my entire family," he said.

I couldn't blame my father for the famine or our troubles. But for the next week, I still couldn't face him. Whenever I did, I saw the rest of my life.

My greatest fear was coming true: I would end up just

like him, another poor Malawian farmer digging the soil. Thin and dirty, with hands as rough as timber and feet that knew no shoes. My life would forever be controlled by rain and the price of fertilizer and seeds—never by me. I would grow maize, and if I was lucky, maybe a little tobacco. And years when the crops were good and there was a little extra to sell, perhaps I could buy a new set of clothes. But most of the time, there would be hardly enough to eat. My future had been chosen, and thinking about it scared me so badly, I wanted to be sick. But what could I do? Nothing, only accept.

I had no time to feel sorry for myself. The maize was finally ready in the fields, and my father needed all of our help. As much as I'd waited for this time to come, I entered the harvest with a conflicted heart. Now that I knew I wasn't going to school, the maize rows appeared like the bars of my own prison. I would enter their shadows and the gates would lock behind me.

But at the same time, my God, we were finally harvesting our food.

And really, the harvest was the most fun time of the year, even better than Christmas. It was a time to celebrate all of your hard work, all the mornings you woke up at four a.m. to dig ridges and pull weeds. But this season, it was even more significant: a time to remember the famine, the many nights of hunger, and the good people across Malawi who didn't survive. Mostly, I thought about Khamba and the sadness I carried inside.

And now as we entered the maize rows, ready to work, it was as if God was rewarding us for our sacrifice. We had a beautiful crop.

"The best in years," my father said. "Just look at it."

My mother stood beside him, staring across the fields with a smile I hadn't seen in months. "We made it after all," she said.

For the next two weeks, we harvested all day with satisfied minds, and at night we slept like lions with bellies full of food. After collecting the cobs and hauling them home by oxcart, we spent three glorious weeks just sitting in the courtyard plucking what we'd grown. We listened to the radio, sang songs, talked about the weather. Life had returned to normal.

In storage, our grain sacks were full once again—so many, they reached the ceiling and spilled out the doorway. Some soybeans from the garden were also ready, which meant we could enjoy regular meals. Slowly, all the weight we'd lost during the famine started coming back.

"Ay, Papa," my mother said to my father one night, "you were looking so *skinny*."

My father smiled. "And you, Mama. I see you're finally coming back to us. But William, *eh*, I was worried that a strong wind would carry that boy away."

We all laughed about it now, because it was only during good times that we could talk truthfully about the bad.

Once harvest was over, I was able to return to the scrap-yard to collect pieces for my windmill. Walking through the tall grass, I'd see something interesting, pick it up, and think, *What on earth is this?* only to spot something even better a second later.

One day while poking through the weeds, I found what looked like a four-wheel-drive differential—the gears that send power to the wheels and allow the vehicle to turn. I managed to pry off the casing with my screwdriver and discovered gobs of black engine grease. *Every machine needs grease*, I thought. I scooped it out into a plastic bag and stuck it in my pocket.

That same day, I found a handful of cotter pins left inside a discarded hubcap. I collected bits of wire, plus some things I'd probably never use—brake pedals, a broken gear stick, and the crankshaft from a small engine. I took them home anyway.

Early on, I realized that one of my biggest, most important pieces—a bicycle—had been sitting under my roof from the start. My father's broken bike had been leaning against the wall of the living room for over a year, collecting dust and dirty laundry. It had no handlebars, only one wheel, and its frame was as rusted as anything in the scrapyard. I'd offered to repair it many times, but my father always gave the same answer: "There's just no money."

One day I finally gathered the courage to ask him if I could use it for my windmill. I sat him down and explained the entire process, how the bike frame would make the perfect body and be sturdy enough to handle strong winds. I described how the wind and blades would act as pedals to spin the wheel and power the generator.

"Electricity!" I said, spreading my arms like a magician. "Water!"

My father just shook his head. "Son, please don't break my bike. I've already lost so many radios. Besides, one day we'll use that thing."

Use it for what? I thought. To ride five miles to buy

kerosene for the lanterns that make us all sick, when you could have lights for free? Oh, it took so long to convince my father to give up that piece of junk. I must have begged for an hour.

"I have a plan!" I persisted. "Allow me to try. Just think, we could have lights! We could pump water and have an extra harvest! We'll never go hungry again."

He considered this a while, then finally gave in. "Okay, perhaps you're right. But please don't mess it up."

I grabbed the bicycle and hurried into my room, where I leaned it against the wall with my other materials. Standing back, I realized how my room had come to resemble the scrapyard itself. All of my windmill pieces—the bicycle, tractor fan, shock absorber, and bearings—sat in a picture-perfect row, like in a museum.

The rest of the floor, however, was covered with random greasy bits that spilled under the bed and piled behind the door. The room smelled like the inside of a transmission. *You never know what you might need*, I reasoned.

Of course, I forbade my sisters from even entering my room to sweep and mop. I was certain they didn't appreciate the value of a used muffler clamp or water pump. Who knows what they might sweep into the dustbin?

"But Mama told us to clean!" they yelled through the door.

"I'll tell you when it's time," I answered. "I'm busy."

When I wasn't in the scrapyard, I hung out at the library or sat in my hammock and read. At this point, my father felt so bad about my schooling that he no longer forced me to work in the fields. This made my sisters jealous.

"Why does William get to stay home and not us?" Doris asked my father one day. "Is it because he's a boy and we're girls? If he's staying home, so are we!"

"William has a project," my father said. "And if he's really wasting time, he'll be proven wrong eventually. You girls just worry about yourselves."

With my father's blessing, I spent mornings and afternoons planning my windmill. I pored over chapters about electricity in *Explaining Physics*. I learned how it moves and behaves and how it can be harnessed. I reviewed sections on home wiring, parallel circuits versus series circuits, and more stuff on AC and DC currents. Back at the library, I renewed the same three books over and over until one day Ms. Sikelo raised her eyebrow.

"William, are you still preparing for exams? What are you up to?"

"Just building something," I said. "You'll see."

⚡

More and more, going to the scrapyard began to replace school in my mind. It was an environment where I learned something new each day. I'd see strange and foreign materials and try to imagine their use. One thing looked like an old compressor, or perhaps it was a landmine. I found real compressors and shook them to hear the pieces rattling inside; then I would pry them open and investigate. My imagination was constantly at work.

Sometimes I pretended to be a great mechanic, crawling on my back under the rusted cars with the tall grass clutching me in its arms. I'd shout up to the customer.

"Start it up! Let's see how she sounds . . . Give it gas, don't be shy! *Whoa, whoa, whoa!* That's too much!"

If the engine didn't sound right, I gave it to them straight:

"Looks like you need an overhaul. I know, I know, it's expensive, but that's life."

I shouted to my other mechanics, who were slacking as usual.

"Phiri, today you're doing oil changes!"

"Yes, boss!"

Another mechanic walked over shaking his head. Problems again.

"Mister Kamkwamba, boss, we can't fix this car. We've

tried everything, but it still makes a noise. What do you think?"

"Start it up. Hmm . . . yes . . . hmm. Injector pump."

"Thank you, sir!"

"For sure."

I climbed atop the tractors, pressed the ignition button with my foot, and pretended to drive. "Out of my way—your man Kamkwamba must work!"

In my mind, I dug ridges in my field, making up for all the days I'd swung a hoe in the sun. Each time, I wished one of those tractors would actually fire up and move. If it did, I'd drag the whole scrapyard home.

But no matter how much fun I had, my mood didn't last long. The students across the street at Kachokolo could see me banging away on various things. If I wasn't careful, they could even hear me talking to myself. A few times while carrying out my pieces, some kids in the playground cried, "Hey look, it's William, digging in the garbage again!"

The first time it happened, I walked over and tried explaining the windmill, but the kids just laughed. Even days when I tried sneaking past, someone would spot me through the open window and shout, "There goes the crazy guy, off to smoke his *chamba*!"

Chamba is marijuana.

Luckily I did have a few supporters. But Geoffrey had been hired by our uncle Musaiwale to work at the maize mill in Chipumba, and that meant that Gilbert was the only person I could trust. Finally I decided that whenever someone shouted, "William, what are you doing in the garbage?" I'd just smile and say nothing.

Of course, the students at Kachokolo told their parents about the lunatic in the scrapyard, and soon my mother was getting an earful in the trading center. Now when I came home with my pieces, she stared at me and shook her head. One day she barged into my room, looking worried.

"What's wrong with you?" she said. "Your friends don't behave this way. I mean, look at this room! It looks like a madman's room. Only madmen collect garbage."

That night she complained to my father, "How is he ever going to find a wife like this? How is he going to care for a family?"

"Leave the boy alone," my father said. "Let's see what he has up his sleeve."

Over the next few weeks, the treasures kept revealing themselves like pieces of a magic puzzle. When I realized

I needed more PVC, Gilbert allowed me to dig up the drainage pipe from the floor of his bathhouse. He didn't bother asking his father, who wasn't happy the next morning.

Once the pipe was cleaned and dry, I cut it down the middle with my bow saw. I melted it over the fire until it bubbled and curled, then rolled it off and pounded it flat. I then cut four blades, each measuring four feet in length.

I wanted to go ahead and connect the blades to my tractor fan, but I had no nuts and bolts. I spent the next two weeks in the scrapyard turning over every machine and piece of metal. But I only had a box-end wrench, and it was too large for most of the bolts I found. Many were so rusted, they stripped against the tool or refused to budge.

I told this pathetic story to Gilbert one afternoon and right away he offered to help. His father sometimes gave him money for working in their fields. That day, Gilbert walked to Mister Daud's shop with fifty kwacha and bought a sack full of screws, bolts, and nuts—all the perfect size for my windmill. I was so grateful.

But I still had a problem: The metal pieces needed to be welded together, to ensure they would hold. We had no welding machine at home, and to hire a welder cost more money. I was stalled again.

Then one day in the trading center, I got lucky. I was playing *bawo* with some friends when a man pulled up in a dump truck. He was from Kasungu and needed boys to help load some wood.

"I'll pay two hundred kwacha for the job," he said.

I ran over waving my arms. "I'll do it, I'll do it!" He motioned me into the truck bed, along with ten other guys. I spent all afternoon throwing logs under the sun—tired, sweaty, and with the biggest grin on my face.

With two hundred kwacha, I could pay a welder for the first phase of work: connecting the shock absorber shaft to the bicycle's bottom bracket. That way it could spin the crankset and chain and move the wheel. I also needed him to melt holes in the metal blades of the tractor fan so I could bolt the bigger PVC blades.

Mister Godsten's shop was in the trading center under a grass-covered shelter. He used an electric welding box, ancient-looking and made from wood, that plugged into the wall of his home with a long, patched-together cord. A crowd of people usually gathered around to watch him weld, myself included. The men would discuss the particular project while the boys played in the shower of sparks that shot from his gun.

Even though I had money for the job, Godsten laughed when I walked up carrying my pieces.

"You want me to weld a broken shock absorber to a bicycle with one wheel?" he asked, mocking me. Others in the crowd joined in.

"Ah, look, the madman has come with his garbage. We've been hearing about you."

"*Eh*, he's not a man—just a lazy boy who plays with toys and refuses to work. He's *misala*."

That means crazy. My face grew hot. I was so tired of hearing those words.

"That's right," I said. "I'm lazy, *misala*, whatever you want to call me. But I have a plan and I know what I'm doing. Soon all of you will see."

I then turned to Godsten and gave him the dead eye.

"And to answer your question, mister," I said, "you heard me right: Weld the shock absorber to the bicycle. And make sure it's not crooked."

When Godsten was finished, I paid him my money and took the bicycle home. I returned it to its place in my room and started laughing. It really did look like a madman's creation: The shock absorber jutted from the crankset like a strange robotic arm, its joints fused with melted metal. Next to it, my blades leaned against the wall like giant insect wings, their white surfaces scorched and bubbled like a burned marshmallow. The tractor fan looked like a super Chinese throwing star—one that would slice through the darkness leaving a trail of light.

I couldn't wait to put them all together.

But once again, I was missing something, and it was a big something. I needed a generator. But where in the world was I going to find such an expensive thing? I could wait and try to earn five hundred kwacha to buy the dynamo in Daud's shop, but that could take forever. The owner of the dry-goods store had hired a permanent team of workers to unload his trucks, and jobs loading wood came only so often.

So I went back to the scrapyard.

I spent the next three weeks sifting through the grass like a bomb-sniffing dog, turning over every piece of metal in hopes of uncovering a generator I may have missed. Or at least an alternator. *Hadn't I seen several of those?* Well, it turned out that I wasn't the only one looking for such things. Some younger boys from the trading center had also discovered the importance of electric motors. But instead of using them for science, they were just stripping out the wire to build toy trucks.

I caught them one day as I entered the yard. I shouted, "Hey you!" but they took off running. Maybe they'd heard stories about the madman and feared for their lives. Anyway, when I got to where they'd been standing, I found a perfectly good motor stripped of its wires. It lay there dead in the grass like one of those poached elephants missing its tusks.

I began to fear my windmill would never get built. Worse, over the next month, it seemed like every dynamo in central Malawi came out to taunt me. I saw them on bicycles everywhere, and most of the time they were broken, not even attached to a bulb. I'd think, *God, what a waste! Give it to me and I'll show you how to use it!* Others worked perfectly and shot fat beams of light down the dark roads at night. I never had the courage to flag down the owners. What would I say?

Instead, I woke up each morning to the pile of metal in my room, then went and helped my father in the fields. At night, the windmill pieces were easier to look at, since everything disappeared in the dark.

One Friday in July, Gilbert and I were walking home from the trading center and I was feeling glum.

"How's the windmill going?" he asked.

"I have everything, but still no generator," I said. "If I had that, I could build it tomorrow. I'm afraid this dream will never come true."

"Oh, sorry, friend."

Just then, we saw a guy pushing his bike. I didn't know him, but he was around our age. And as he passed, I looked down and noticed a familiar glitter by his tire.

"And look," I said, "another dynamo."

But this time I wasn't afraid. I ran over to the guy and asked if I could see his bike. I bent down and gave the pedal a good spin, and when I did, the headlamp—an old car bulb—flickered on.

Gilbert turned to him. "How much to buy the dynamo?" he asked.

"No, Gilbert," I said, "I don't have any—"

"How much?" Gilbert said again.

The guy refused at first, but finally gave in. No one was foolish enough to refuse money at this time. "Two hundred kwacha," he said, "with the bulb."

"I still have some money from my father," Gilbert told me. "Let's use it to buy the dynamo. Let's finish the windmill!"

He reached into his pocket and pulled out two hundred kwacha—two red paper notes. After some messing around to get the dynamo and bulb off the bike, I was holding them in my hand.

"*Zikomo kwa mbiri*, Gilbert," I said. "Thank you very much. You're the greatest friend I ever had."

While Gilbert went home, I ran back to my room and placed the dynamo with the other materials, adding the last piece of the puzzle. The moment I laid it down, a magnificent gust of wind blew open my door and spun a cyclone into the room. It whipped up the windmill pieces in its arms and revealed the finished machine, its blades spinning wildly through the blur of red dust. Or maybe that was only a dream.

CHAPTER ELEVEN
THE WINDMILL COMES TO LIFE

The following afternoon, I began assembling the machine.

I dragged the bicycle, tractor fan, blades, bolts, and dynamo outside and arranged them along the dirt. I'd chosen an area behind the kitchen, which doubled as my laboratory. The acacia tree provided plenty of shade against the midmorning sun, and I'd also determined it was the ideal place to catch the eastern winds that rushed over the highlands from the lake.

The first thing I wanted to do was connect the blades to the tractor fan. This called for a drill. So I went into the kitchen and stuck the cob-handled nail into the fire, and once it glowed hot, I bored a square pattern of four holes into the top of each plastic blade, plus two more in the center. This process of heating, melting, and reheating took nearly three hours.

Next, I emptied the sack of nuts and bolts that Gilbert had given me onto the ground and started to fasten the first blade. That's when I realized I'd forgotten the washers.

"Ah!" I shouted, frustrated with myself.

Well, I definitely needed washers to secure the bolts, so I spent the next hour collecting bottle caps outside Ofesi Boozing Centre. Once I had about twenty, I hurried home, hammered them flat, and used a nail to poke a hole through their middles. *Perfect*.

One by one, I drove bolts through each washer and tightened the nuts, until all four blades were connected. Lastly, I wanted to make sure the blades were strong and wouldn't snap in a heavy wind. So I wired three-foot bamboo reinforcements to each one, to where they acted like bones.

"Okay now," I said. "Let's have a look."

I stood back to examine my work. From end to end,

the wingspan of the blades stretched more than eight feet, causing me to giggle with excitement.

It was then that I noticed the compound was empty. My sisters were off running errands and my father was attending a funeral in a nearby village. Besides my clinking and hammering, the only other noise was my mother humming to herself in the kitchen as she prepared a pot of beans for our supper. The privilege of privacy was mine, and I fell into deep concentration.

The next thing was to figure out how to connect everything to the bicycle, which wasn't going to be easy. I started by steadying the blades atop four tall bricks—like how a mechanic puts a car on blocks—so I would have some room to work underneath. Then came the hard part. The bicycle was not only heavy, but cumbersome, especially with a giant shock absorber sticking out from the crankset. But I managed to lift it high enough to flip it over, then dropped the shock absorber into the center hole of the tractor fan. Quickly, I crouched down underneath the bricks and jammed a cotter pin through the other end, locking it tight.

Finally, I attached the dynamo to the bike frame so its metal wheel hugged against the sidewall of the tire. I strung the chain, which was coated in warm, black grease, over the crankset and made sure it held tight against the sprockets.

By the time I finished the chain, the sun was setting behind the trees and soon it would be too dark to work. I packed my tools away in my room, then moved the windmill against the wall of the kitchen and out of the way. I drew a bucket of water from the well and heated it for my bath, and after bathing, headed inside for supper. By then my sister Rose had returned from the shops and saw me in the courtyard.

"William, we haven't seen you all day," she said. "People in the trading center were asking about you."

"Well, today your brother was busy," I said.

"I told them you were playing with your metals to make power."

"Something like that," I said, smiling. "Just wait. Soon you'll be in for a surprise, along with everyone else."

I ate my supper like a real working man, saying nothing except to utter a few well-orchestrated grunts. When I finished eating, I returned to my room, lay down on my bed, and was asleep in seconds.

The following morning, I was awake at first light and ready to continue.

My plan was to build a tall wooden tower for the windmill, but first I had to see if it even worked. For this, I needed something temporary. So I found a thick piece of bamboo, more than six inches wide, and bored a hole through the top, then drove the other end into the dirt.

I finished just in time to see Geoffrey ride up on his bicycle from Chipumba. It happened to be his day off and he was coming to visit me.

"*Eh*, man, just in time," I said.

"Is this the same project you were working on?"

"*Yah*, this is everything. I'm glad you're here, friend. Help me lift this thing."

We locked up the bicycle wheel and chain to keep them from spinning, then carefully hoisted the machine onto the pole. I was out of rope, so once it felt sturdy, Geoffrey secured it using long strips from an inner tube.

"Shall we?" he asked.

"We shall."

Geoffrey unlocked the tire so the blades could spin, except we didn't realize how quickly this would happen. In Malawi, the wind is never still. Within seconds, the blades were spinning so fast, the chain snapped in half and the pole nearly tipped over.

"Hold it!" I shouted.

Geoffrey and I barely managed to catch the machine before it crashed to the ground and broke apart. Once we had a grip, I twisted the pole and turned the blades out of the wind's direction. Then I spent the next two hours fixing the chain.

The main reason for the test was to see if the dynamo produced enough current. I already knew it could power a small bicycle lamp, but what else? I went to my father's room and grabbed his International radio, which was forbidden to me, given my history with the family's other electronics. When I returned, Geoffrey gave me a look.

"Does your father know you're borrowing this?" he asked.

I waved him off. "He's in the trading center. He'll never know it was gone."

I jammed the dynamo's two wires into the radio's AC socket and Geoffrey unlocked the windmill blades. They began to twirl and the dynamo's metal wheel zipped against the spinning tire. For the slightest moment, I heard music. It worked! But a second later, black smoke started to pour out of the speakers.

"Oh no!" Geoffrey said, and ripped out the wires. The radio sat on the ground between us, sizzling like an egg.

He spun around, looking for my father, but I was too excited to care.

"Did you see that power?" I screamed, jumping up and down. "Did you see it?"

The radio blew up because the dynamo produced too many volts of electricity. Voltage, as I'd learned in my books, is how you measure electrical pressure. Think of it like the water pressure coming out of a hose. The dynamo produced twelve volts when someone was pedaling like normal. This was enough for a radio or lightbulb to manage. But when the wind gusted and spun the blades like mad, it caused a power surge that increased the voltage and fried my father's radio. I had to figure out how to reduce it.

I flipped through *Explaining Physics* to where it showed a diagram of two separate lightbulbs, both being lit from a low, twelve-volt AC supply—exactly like my dynamo. Both bulbs were connected by long wires. One bulb burned very bright, all because of something called a transformer, which boosted the voltage and made it stronger. But the second bulb didn't have a transformer and glowed dim and yellow. That's because without the transformer, power was lost in the form of heat on its journey through the wires—something called dissipation.

"Mister Geoffrey," I said, "since energy can be lost in the wires when traveling long distances, perhaps we can try this on the dynamo."

I went into our big pile of radio parts and found an old motor. I cracked it open, removed the core, and unwound the long copper wire. I then wrapped it around a stick, creating my own kind of reverse transformer. I attached one end of the wire to the dynamo, and the other end to my father's radio, which somehow managed to survive the power surge. Just like in the book, I was giving the electricity an extra-long road to travel, hoping some of its voltage would get lost along the way.

"Okay, try it again," I said to Geoffrey. He unlocked the blades, and the wheel and dynamo began to whir. This time, there was only music. Our test was complete.

The windmill sat on the bamboo pole for two days, hidden behind the house and out of sight. In the meantime, Geoffrey, Gilbert, and I set out to build a real tower. The three of us met in front of my house one morning with our panga machetes and walked into the blue-gum forest.

It was the same grove of trees where I'd sought refuge from the bubble-gum curse and where I'd accepted

Shabani's magic, only to be beaten that day in Dowa. And now it was where I went to build my ladder to science.

We walked through the forest, looking carefully at each tree. Finally, we chose one that was about eighteen feet high. We tore into the trunk with our blades, and after ten minutes, the tree crashed to the ground. We used our pangas to prune the branches, then stripped the thin bark with our hands. By three o'clock, we'd felled and cleaned two additional trees and were hoisting them onto our shoulders, headed home.

Just behind the kitchen, we set the poles deep into the ground, each one the same distance from the other. Each pole was wrapped in *jumbo* bags to keep out the termites.

We took smaller branches and nailed them sideways like rungs of a ladder, using nails that Geoffrey had bought using his pay from the maize mills. By sundown, the tower was complete. It stood fifteen feet high and was remarkably sturdy. However, from just a short distance away, its long and spindly legs gave it the appearance of a wobbly giraffe.

"Get some sleep, gents," I said. "Tomorrow we raise the machine."

⁂

I could barely sleep that night and was out the door before the rooster even crowed. When I rounded the kitchen, Gilbert and Geoffrey were already standing by the tower.

"Look who decided to sleep late," Geoffrey said.

I was so happy to see them.

The windmill's frame weighed about ninety pounds, and the only way to hoist it up the tower was by rope and pulley. I didn't have any rope, so I had to borrow my mother's wire clothesline instead. I fastened one end to a crude handle that I'd made on the windmill from a piece of bamboo. I climbed the tower with the other end and looped it over the top rung, then dropped it down to Gilbert. From where I stood, I could see over the trees to where the patchwork of fields and forest joined the highlands.

"Okay, Gilbert," I yelled. "Bring it up."

Slowly, he began to pull. The bamboo handle lifted in the air, followed by the large gangly frame.

"Easy now!"

Geoffrey stood below me on a lower rung to guide the machine as it climbed. The three of us now pulled with all our strength.

"Come on, guys!" I shouted. "Let's see those muscles!"

"I'm pulling as hard as I can," said Gilbert, straining under the weight.

"Don't let it slip, Geoffrey!"

With each pull, the windmill lurched sideways and banged its cumbersome blades against the wood. A couple of times they got stuck in the rungs and Geoffrey had to knock them loose. Little by little, it made its way up the tower.

After half an hour, we finally had it close to the top. When it came within reach, I grabbed the handle and screamed to Gilbert: "Tie it down!"

Gilbert looped the wire around the base pole, and the windmill held. Geoffrey joined me at the top to secure the machine in place.

The day before, we'd drilled two holes in the wooden poles. My hot-nail drill wasn't big enough, so I had to use flat bolts instead, a process that took hours. We'd also asked Mister Godsten to cut two matching holes in the bicycle's crossbar with his welding gun.

Standing atop the tower, Geoffrey fished the nuts and bolts from his pocket while I held the frame and tried to align the holes. I could feel it slipping.

"Hurry, this thing is heavy!" I said.

Geoffrey slid in the bolts and tightened them with the wrench. Once everything was fastened, we looked at each other and smiled. The machine felt sturdy and very strong.

While Geoffrey made his way down the tower, I remained atop my perch to take in the scenery. To the north, I could see the iron-sheet roofs of the trading center and the rows of brown huts that sat behind the market. As I admired the view, I noticed something strange: A line of people had emerged and were heading in my direction. They must have seen the tower from the distance and were curious to have a look.

"We have visitors," I said.

Within minutes, a dozen people gathered at the base and gazed up at the machine. I recognized a few of them as traders and shopkeepers. One was named Kalino.

"What is this thing?" he asked.

Since there's no word in Chichewa for windmill, I used the phrase *magesti a mphepo*. "Electric wind," I answered.

"What does it do?"

"Generates electricity from the wind."

"That's impossible," Kalino said, laughing. He turned to get a reaction from the crowd. "It looks like a radio tower, and what kind of silly toy is that?"

"Well," I said, "just stand back and watch."

I climbed down from the tower and ran into my room for the final piece. That morning I'd found a thick reed and cut a section about ten inches long. I then wrapped a long copper wire around the base of a headlamp bulb and strung it through, creating a light socket.

Holding the socket and bulb, I climbed the tower and connected their wires to the ones from the dynamo. As I worked, more and more people arrived and I could hear their chatter:

"What do you suppose he's doing now?" asked a farmer named Banda.

"This is the *misala* from the scrapyard my children were talking about," another man answered. "Think about his poor mother!"

Peering out, I saw my parents and sisters at the back of the crowd. Their eyes were wide and their jaws hung slightly open, the way some soccer fans look when clustered around a radio. Except this time, it was me who had the ball with only seconds left on the clock. My hands trembled from nerves, but I was confident. I'd prepared for this moment for months.

"Let's see how crazy this boy really is," I heard someone shout.

A steady wind whistled through the tower, mixing the smells of chain grease and melted plastic. Even though the wheel remained locked, the machine groaned against the breeze, as if begging me to release it. I looked down at Gilbert and Geoffrey and nodded.

Here it goes, I thought.

I jerked the wheel loose and the blades began to spin. The chain snapped tight against the crankset and the tire slowly turned. Everything happened in slow motion.

"Come on," I said. "Don't embarrass me now."

Just then a strong gust flung me backward. The tower began to rock, so much that I wrapped my elbow around a rung just to hang on. Inches above my head, the blades began to buzz like a set of angry propellers. I clutched the bulb, waiting for my miracle.

Then it came: a flicker, a flash, then a burst of bright, magnificent light. My heart nearly exploded.

"Look!" someone shouted. "He's made light!"

"It's true what he said!"

A group of children pushed through the crowd.

"Look how it spins!"

"Let me see!"

I threw my hands into the air and shouted with joy, laughing so hard that I became dizzy. I held the bulb in triumph and addressed the unbelievers:

"Electric wind!" I shouted. "I told you I wasn't mad!"

One by one, the people began to cheer. They waved their hands and shouted, "*Wachitabwina*! Well done!"

"You did it, William!"

"That's right," I said. "And now I'm going bigger! Just wait and see!"

The crowd shouted questions, then gathered around Gilbert and Geoffrey, grilling them for details. Those two guys couldn't stop grinning. I stayed on the tower listening to the blades and taking in the scene. I finally came down when the bulb started to burn my hand.

My wire wasn't long enough to use the bulb anywhere but the windmill. So late in the afternoon, I attached it to the top rung and left it. I was still so high from the experience that I went to the trading center to burn off some energy and relish in the glory. Once I reached the market stalls, I looked back to the valley and saw the light still flickering through the heat waves.

"What is that thing?" said a man nearby, clutching a sack of tomatoes. "It's catching the wind just like a helicopter."

The tomato seller was my mother's friend Maggie. "Well, the owner is right here. Why don't you ask him?"

"Is this true?" he said. "How is that possible?"

I explained it to him the way I did everyone.

"I still don't understand," he said. "I need to come see for myself."

For the next month, about thirty people arrived each day to stare up at the light.

"How did you manage such a thing?" they all asked.

"Hard work and lots of research," I replied, trying not to sound too smug.

Many of them were traveling businessmen from other districts. To them, the windmill became a kind of road-side attraction while passing through Wimbe. Other people came from outer villages with chickens and maize strapped to their bicycles. Women balancing sacks of flour on their heads stopped and spoke with my mother.

"God has blessed you," one said. "You have a child who can perform wonders. You'll never complain about kerosene again."

The men approached my father.

"Your son made this?"

"Yes."

"Where did he get such ideas?"

"From books."

"They teach this in school?"

"No, he did this on his own."

That month I helped clear the fields and prepare them

for planting, working each day with joy in my heart. If I was in the fields near the windmill, I would pause in between swings of my hoe and just watch it spin.

One night I was playing *bawo* with Geoffrey and Gilbert near the barber shop when the lights went out from a power cut. While everyone was cursing the dark, I snuck home and connected the bulb, then ran back.

"Oh, I hate these power cuts!" a man complained, leaving the barber shop with only half a haircut.

"What power cuts?" I said with a smile. "Have you chaps seen my house?"

Mister Iponga, the barber, leaned out his shop, still clutching his dead clippers. "William, I think you take pride in our power cuts just so you can boast about your electric wind."

"Perhaps."

The next month, I started working on lighting my house using the windmill. To do this, I needed loads and loads of electrical wire. But as usual, I had no money to buy any. Then one afternoon, Gilbert and I were at Charity's house when I noticed long sections of copper-insulated wire—the very kind I needed—being used as clothing line. In fact, a whole spool of the stuff sat in the corner of the room.

"*Eh*, man," I said to Charity, "how can you play around with this wire when I need it so much?"

Someone had given it to him as payment for *ganyu*, he said.

"But since you're my cousin, I'll give you a discount."

I was on my way to the trading center to look for a job when Gilbert pulled out one hundred kwacha and gave it to Charity. Just like that, I had thirty meters of copper wire.

"I promise I'll pay you back, Gilbert," I said.

"Don't worry about it. Just put lights in your room."

Once again, when all hope seemed lost, Gilbert came to the rescue.

I ran toward home clutching the heavy spool. As I flew down the trail and into the valley, I could see the windmill spinning in the distance. Now every time I saw it, my stomach did a flip.

I unspooled the wire enough to measure the distance from the windmill to my room, then clipped it with my knife. Clutching one end, I climbed the tower.

A windmill in motion was a hazardous work environment. The blades were spinning so fast, I had to be careful, or else I'd end up with a haircut. Also, the dynamo was producing real electricity. As I unhooked the bulb and attached the new wire, I was mindful not to cross them or I'd get a shock. To be extra safe, I wrapped a *jumbo* bag—which is plastic and doesn't conduct electricity—around the junction where the wires tied together.

The roof of my bedroom was made from pallets of grass wrapped in plastic sheeting, each supported by several wooden beams. Standing on a ladder, I wrapped the wire two turns around the middle beam—the one nearest my bed—then popped a hole through the pallet and lowered it down into my room.

Inside, I made some final attachments, then pulled the bulb from my pocket. *I may not be touching the wall to get light*, I thought, thinking back to Gilbert's light switch, *but this is close enough*. I connected the reed and bulb, and in an instant, my room was illuminated. I ran to the door and slammed it closed, then marveled at the new electricity. For the first time ever, I had my own lighted space.

That evening after supper, I lay in bed and just stared up at the bulb. It flickered yellow to the rhythm of the spinning blades outside, bright enough to read the library books I'd stacked up around me.

I heard a knock at the door and soon my family had crowded into my room.

"Look, it's William staying up past the dark," my father said.

"Congratulations," said my mother. "We'd also like to have lights in our rooms. Think you can manage?"

"Only if you're okay with having electricity generated by a madman."

She laughed. "*Eh*, you proved us all wrong in the end. But I'll admit, I did worry."

My sister Rose then asked, "What if the wind stops blowing?"

It was an important question. "The light will go off," I said. "And I'll be stranded. That's why I have plans for getting some batteries."

More specifically, I needed something like a car battery so I could store power for the times when the wind was calm. A car battery was also big enough to power the entire house. Once I had one, my family could finally toss out those kerosene lamps and live like modern people.

And lights were just the first step. The next windmill would pump water for our fields and give us more food. Windmills would be our front line against hunger.

That first night with light, I stayed awake reading

Explaining Physics, trying to prepare for my next step. I read for hours, long after everyone else was asleep, while the termites feasted on the roof and clouds of red dust pushed under the door. As usual, a strong wind was blowing.

CHAPTER TWELVE
BIGGER AND BRIGHTER

As I explained to Rose, without wind, there was no light. On calm, still nights, we were stuck in the dark with our kerosene lanterns. The only way to change this was by finding a car battery. But until one came along, I found other uses for the windmill—like charging mobile phones.

I discovered this when my cousin Ruth visited from Muzuzu. Ruth was Uncle Socrates' oldest daughter, who was married and had a good job. She also had a cell phone she was always bugging me to charge down at the trading center.

Some guys in the market were making loads of money

charging phones for people who had no electricity in their homes. They cut deals with shopkeepers, who allowed them to run long extension cords to the roadside, where they set up a little stall. They sold scratch cards with airtime minutes, and some even had mobile phones that people could use to make calls—like a pay phone. I later discovered that these kinds of stalls are found all over Africa. In bigger cities, such as Nairobi, Lilongwe, and Kinshasa, some guys even powered photocopiers, computers, and printers this way, letting people prepare their work résumés and call about jobs—all on the sidewalk. Of course, the frequent blackouts in these cities were never good for business.

Anyway, one day I was complaining about having to take Ruth's phone to the trading center when she said, "Why don't you charge it with your windmill. It produces electricity, right?"

I'd already considered this, but the dynamo didn't generate enough voltage to power a phone. It produced twelve volts—which was fine for lightbulbs and smaller things—when a charger needed two hundred twenty.

If you remember, while testing the radio, I'd discovered that energy decreases when passing through wire over long distances. But to charge a phone, I'd need something to boost the power—something called a step-up transformer.

Electric companies across the world, especially in Europe and America, "step up" power all the time. Because electricity gets lost on the journey from the power station to your home, the company installs transformers along the way that add that extra boost. It's like giving your electricity some coffee and doughnuts to keep it going.

A step-up transformer has two coils—the primary and secondary—located on either side of a core. Alternating current flows back and forth and causes the primary coil to induce a charge in the second coil. This process is called mutual induction, which means that voltage from one coil jumps into another. The result is that the overall voltage increases. I learned this from *Explaining Physics* in a chapter entitled "Mutual Induction and Transformers," which showed a picture of a man with white hair and a bow tie. This was Michael Faraday, who invented the first transformer in 1831. *Cheers to that guy*, I thought.

Using the diagrams, I was determined to make my own step-up transformer. First, I borrowed a pair of wire cutters and cut an iron sheet into an *E* pattern. The diagram showed how to boost twenty-four volts into two hundred twenty. It explained how voltage increased with each turn of the wire, how the primary coil needed two hundred turns, while the secondary needed two thousand. Next to it was a bunch of mathematical equations, but I paid them no mind. I started wrapping like mad and hoped it worked.

I then connected the dynamo wires to the primary coil, while the secondary coil was wired directly to the prongs of a phone charger. Ruth stood over me, eyebrows raised.

"Don't blow it up," she said.

I lied, "I know what I'm doing."

When I plugged in the phone jack, the screen brightened and the bars began moving up and down. It worked!

"See? I told you."

To make things easier, I built a plug using the AC outlet from an old radio, which I fixed into the wall like a normal electric socket. When news of this invention reached the trading center, the line of people wanting to charge their phones reached the road.

Many people who came still pretended to not believe me—probably in hopes that I wouldn't charge them money.

They said, "Are you *sure* this electric wind can charge my phone?"

"I'm positive."

"Prove it."

"See, it charges."

"My God, you're right. But leave it for a little longer. I'm still not convinced."

After two months of using this method, I finally went bigger. I was over at Charity's one day and spotted an actual car battery sitting in the corner.

"I found it yesterday on the road," he said. "Just pay me when you can."

From studying my books, I knew that car batteries used DC power. So if I wanted to charge it using my dynamo—which spit out AC power—I'd have to find a way to convert it. My book talked about diodes, or rectifiers, which are found in many radios and electronic devices and convert this power for you.

The kind of diode I needed looked like a tiny D-cell battery on a long metal skewer. The sight of it reminded me of the smoked-mice kebobs that boys sold along the highway as snacks. After studying the picture, I easily found one inside an old six-volt radio in Geoffrey's room. I fashioned a soldering iron from a piece of heated cable, then fused the diode to the wire between the windmill and car battery.

Kamkwamba, I thought to myself, *you are one clever chap!*

But not so fast, because doing this created a new kind of problem: the phone-charging plug in my wall only worked with AC power. I puzzled over this for several days and searched every book for the answer. Finally my cousin Ruth solved it in the simplest of ways. She gave me a phone charger that plugs inside your car—one that uses DC power. After making some modifications to the wires, I had a new wall jack.

With the phone charger out of the way, I now focused on the bigger task of lighting. Armed with the car battery, I was able to install three additional bulbs in the house. I couldn't use normal incandescent bulbs because they only work with AC power, so I had to find alternatives.

At Mister Daud's shop, I found three car bulbs: a brake light and two front headlights. I kept the dynamo bulb in my room (which worked on both AC and DC power). I installed one car bulb above my door outside, one in my parents' bedroom, and another in the living room. When the battery was fully charged, the lights could work for three days without wind.

The bulbs connected directly to the battery with wires and operated on a parallel circuit. I learned about this from *Explaining Physics*, which demonstrated two kinds of circuits: parallel and series.

In a series circuit, one wire connects every bulb to the battery (or whatever power source you're using) in a single path. To complete the circuit, all of the bulbs need to be working. If one burns out, then none of them will work. Some types of Christmas lights used to be this way.

"Where several bulbs have to be powered by a single battery, as in a car lighting system," the book explained, "the usual practice is to connect the bulbs in parallel."

The book showed how the homes in Britain are wired this way. Each bulb is connected with separate wires and has its own circuit. If one bulb burns out, the rest will still work. It went on to say that "bulbs arranged in parallel can have independent switches." A diagram on the next page illustrated the basic design for a light switch. It seemed easy enough, so I built my own using bicycle spokes and strips of iron. For the toggles, or switch, I wanted a good nonconductive material that I could shape the way I wanted. So taking my knife, I carved out several round buttons from a pair of old flip-flops, then mounted them inside small boxes I'd made from melted PVC pipe.

I rigged my switch like I'd seen in the books, with a

wire leading from the power supply to the bulb and the switch in between to complete—or break—the circuit. It was simple: Whenever I pushed the flip-flop button, the spoke and iron connected the terminals.

"Finally," I said, "I can touch the wall and get light!"

Not long after wiring the house, I walked into the living room one night and found my family sitting together. My mother was busy crocheting a beautiful orange tablecloth, while my father and sisters were engrossed in a news program on Radio One. I pretended to be one of the reporters and barged in with my microphone, speaking in a deep, serious voice.

"I'm standing in the living room of the Honorable Mister Kamkwamba. Sir, this room used to be so dark and sad at this hour. Now look at you, enjoying electricity like a city person."

"Oh," my father said, smiling, "enjoying it more than a city person."

"You mean because there are no blackouts and you owe ESCOM nothing?"

"Well, yes," he said. "But also, because my own son made it."

⁂

Having lights in my home was a remarkable improvement, but it also had its problems. My battery and wires were not the best quality, and in fact, they were kind of scary.

I'd used up all of the good copper wire that Charity had given me, so all I had left were bits of stuff I'd found in the scrapyard and trash bins. Some of this wire was never meant to conduct electricity, but I used it anyway. I tied all the pieces together until it looked like one of those escape ropes that prisoners fashioned from bedsheets. It wasn't covered in plastic insulation, either, like true electrical wire, so it sparked whenever I touched it to the battery. I had strung this mangy network to the walls and ceiling (which was made from wood and grass) trying not to cross any wires and send my whole house up in flames.

To make matters worse, the termites were having a party in the wooden beams in my ceiling. Each night, I went to bed listening to the sounds of their tiny jaws, and woke up the next morning to piles of sawdust on the floor. Their ferocious appetites had finally hollowed the beams and caused them to sag. It wasn't long before this nearly caused a disaster.

After a big storm one afternoon, I returned from Geoffrey's house and discovered the beam had finally snapped, probably from the wind. The ceiling now caved in the middle and my floor was covered in dirt and grass. The broken beam had also dumped hundreds of squirming termites onto the floor and across my bed.

At first I tried sweeping them off, but there were too many. My father had managed to buy a few more chickens, and as I looked out my open door, I saw a gang of them walking past.

"Come here, chickens," I called out. "Do I have a treat for you!"

I tossed a few termites out the door to lure them in. Once they realized what a great bounty awaited them inside my room, they went crazy with hunger. Soon my floor and bed were filled with chickens, squawking and flapping their wings as they pecked the helpless insects.

This incident caused such a commotion that I didn't even notice the burnt smell. After the chickens cleared out, I looked closely at the broken beam and saw that my wires had crossed during the collapse. Luckily, they were so cheap and thin, they'd simply melted and snapped in two. I thanked God that no one had been hurt.

When Geoffrey arrived later to help pick up the mess, I told him, "It's a good thing I'm too poor to buy quality wire. If I'd used anything better, I'd have burned up my home."

"I warned you about that roof," he said.

"Sure, sure, but I didn't listen."

I needed a proper wiring system, so as always, I turned to *Explaining Physics* for ideas. On page 271, I found a good model. A diagram showed a utility system in a home in England, wired in parallel like mine. After the wires left the power supply, they entered a fuse box, whose job was to shut down the circuit if it ever overloaded. I needed something like this.

The fuses contained tiny metal filaments that melted whenever the overload occurred. But I didn't have any of these, nor did I want them, as the fuses had to be replaced each time. The book went on to describe a similar device called a circuit breaker, which used switches that could be reset. They didn't offer a drawing, but the concept seemed similar to an electric bell, which I'd studied in detail.

In most parts of the world, electric bells are found all over the place, at schools and railroad crossings, in fire alarms, and at one time, in telephones. The concept is amazingly simple, which is why I loved it so much.

It works like this: A coil becomes magnetized and pulls a metal hammer that strikes a gong. That's it. However, during this striking motion, the hammer also trips a switch that breaks the circuit. It does this about a dozen times per second, giving the bell its ring.

I started by making a breaker box from PVC pipe. Next, I wrapped the heads of two nails with copper wire to create two electromagnetic coils. I mounted these inside the box, with the coils facing each other about five inches apart. Coming up between them, I wired a small bar magnet (which I'd busted off a radio speaker) to a piece of bicycle spoke, to where it looked like a lollipop. This magnet lollipop could tick-tock, back and forth, between the two coiled nails.

I then removed the little spring from a ballpoint pen and stretched it out. I positioned it between the lollipop magnet and nail to where it rested lightly against the wire leading to the battery. Basically, this spring completed the circuit and acted as a kind of trap.

When the light was turned on like normal, the electricity flowed from the battery into this circuit and magnetized my two nail coils—one of which was slightly closer to the lollipop. The polarity is determined by which direction the current runs, so I wrapped the nails with wire so the closest one to the lollipop pushed, while the other nail pulled. This pushing and pulling kept the lollipop balanced in the center, never knowing what to do.

In the event of a power surge, the balance would be broken. The coil closer to the lollipop would receive the surge first and push it hard against the other coil, knocking the pen spring loose and breaking the circuit.

As you can imagine, this was tricky to build. I spent hours trying to position the coil and lollipop magnets just right, and determine the best place for the trip wire. Once it was finally done, I nailed the breaker box to my wall just above the battery. Each night I sat on my bed and stared at it, waiting for it to work.

I got my wish about two weeks later when a cyclone hit my house.

I'd spent all day in the trading center, and returned to find bits and pieces of my thatch roof lying in the yard. When my mother came out from the kitchen, I asked what happened.

"A big cyclone just came from the fields. We had to run inside."

I entered my room and saw that the roof had collapsed. Parts of the ceiling were all over the floor. I also noticed that the circuit breaker had flipped, and the lollipop was now stuck against one of the coils. I tried moving it back to the middle, but it refused and just kept swinging back into the nail. After disconnecting the battery,

I followed my wires along the ceiling and discovered they'd become tangled in the cyclone winds. Once I separated them and reconnected the battery, the lollipop returned to the center. Once again, I'd narrowly escaped a fire.

But of course, I was more excited about my circuit breaker than anything.

"Mister Geoffrey, do you realize what this means? My house would be ashes right now. All of my clothes and blankets and books—everything would be gone. My circuit breaker saved the day!"

"Your circuit breaker is great," he agreed. "But I think the better solution is to fix your roof."

Any new invention is going to have problems, and aside from the patchy wiring, one of my biggest headaches was the bike chain. Whenever the wind blew really hard and spun the blades, the chain would snap or simply jump off the teeth of the crankset, forcing me to climb the tower to fix it. This required stopping the blades, which was always painful.

One morning I was enjoying a deep sleep when a terrible racket forced me awake. The chain had broken again. I heard the wind whipping the tree and my tower rocking back and forth. I could tell the blades were spinning so fast, they were buzzing on the rotor. If I didn't fix them soon, they could snap off and fly through the air like daggers.

Outside, I climbed the first set of rungs, and as usual, kicked off my flip-flops so I could get a better grip. But the wind was violent and angry, rocking the tower so hard that I thought it would tip. Looking up, I saw the chain dancing loose over the crankset while the blades spun wild. When I reached the top, I wrapped my legs around the rungs for support. But in trying to keep my balance, I didn't see the bicycle frame swing toward me. Before I could react, the wind sent the blades straight into my hand. The impact knocked me off my feet, and I barely managed to hold on. Looking down, all I saw was blood. Three of my knuckles were now missing their skin.

"You are my own creation!" I shouted to my windmill. "So why are you trying to destroy me? Please, let me help you."

From my pocket, I pulled a strip of bicycle tire that I'd brought for such repairs. I wrapped it around my palm like a protective glove, held my breath, and grabbed hold of the spinning sprocket. The jagged teeth cut into the rubber like a saw blade.

"Stop!"

Once everything was still, I shoved a bent bicycle spoke into the wheel to keep the machine from spinning, then reattached the chain. A few days later, when it happened again, I wasn't so lucky. The teeth on the sprocket cut through the tire rubber and ripped my flesh. Then it happened again. My hands are covered in scars.

During this time, Geoffrey was still working with Uncle Musaiwale at the maize mill in Chipumba. He'd been hired to sweep the floor and fetch things for the business. But once Geoffrey arrived, our uncle would disappear into town and make him run the mill on his own. It was hard and thankless work. About once a month, he came home and complained about his new life as a working man.

"He forces me to ride my bike up five hills to get diesel," Geoffrey said. "And on the way back, the fuel soaks my clothes. I'm telling you, brother, I'm missing you guys terribly."

But he also described how the grinding machines in the mill worked by using pulleys and rubber belts.

"You can solve your chain problem if you use a belt. We use them at the mill, and they never fail."

This was great news. A pulley was just what I needed to increase the tension between the front and back sprockets of the crankset, which was the reason the chain kept flying off. Also, a belt didn't require constant grease.

In the scrapyard, I easily found two pulleys from an old water-pumping engine. I used a piece of heavy steel to snap their cotter pins and slide them off the machine. But the center hole of the larger pulley was too big for my shaft, so I had to weld it alongside the sprocket itself.

These days, Mister Godsten no longer made fun of me. Whenever he saw me walking up holding these random pieces, he just smiled and fired his torch.

"Tell me where."

Mister Godsten even let me use his grinder to flatten all those sharp teeth on the sprocket until its edges were smooth.

"This is for all my scars!" I said as they disappeared under a shower of sparks.

The pulleys worked great, but I didn't have a proper belt. Geoffrey had promised to try and bring me one. But in the meantime, I cut the handle off an old nylon bag and rigged it around the pulleys. It worked for about ten seconds before slipping off. I even cut open a few batteries and removed the ammonium chloride jelly (which I'd first read about in my books), hoping it would act as a glue. But it wore away after a few hours.

An old man in the trading center then gave me an actual belt from a milling machine, which he used to fasten vegetables to his bike. The belt was broken, so I tried mending it with my crochet needle and carbon fiber from a truck tire. It didn't last long. But with nothing else, I used this system for two months.

Finally, Geoffrey returned from Chipumba with a good belt that worked beautifully. At last, no more injuries on the job. Even better, no more getting out of bed in the mornings to climb the tower. Instead, when the rooster stirred me from my dreams in the early morning—which he always did—the steady hum of the machine sang me back to sleep. But sometimes that rooster was a persistent guy, and not even my windmill could guarantee my rest.

"*Chicken!*" I screamed. "If you don't shut up, it'll be your skinny neck spinning from those blades!"

"COCK-A-DOODLE-DOOOOOO!!!!"

It was no use. Conquering darkness on the farm was hard enough, but a noisy chicken—that was impossible.

CHAPTER THIRTEEN
THE RESTLESS INVENTOR

That January, the students returned to school at Kachokolo. I sat on the road one morning listening to them laugh and joke and talk about their friends and teachers, and when they had passed, I went to my room and closed the door.

I still saw Gilbert and the others for games of *bawo*, and when they said things like, "So William, when shall we see you at school again?" or boasted about their grades, I said nothing, or simply told them, "I'd rather not talk about it." After a while, no one did.

It was around then I started noticing the ghosts. Not real ghosts, but boys who'd dropped out of school and now loitered in the trading center without purpose. I'd see them outside the dry-goods store in their bare feet and grimy clothes, waiting for small jobs so they could spend all night in the barrooms.

In Malawi, we say these people are "grooving" through life, just living off *ganyu* with no plans for the future. I started worrying that soon I'd become like them. I worried that one day the windmill would no longer excite me, or it would become too difficult to maintain, and the maize rows or boozing dens would slowly swallow me up. It was easy to lose hold of your dreams.

I battled this darkness by trying to keep a positive mindset. Every week I returned to the library just to continue learning and stay inspired. I read all the novels and spelling books and practiced my English. And I continued checking out *Explaining Physics*, *Using Energy*, and *Integrated Science* and researching other ways to help my family.

Because the windmill had been such a success, I was feeling pressure to do something bigger. I began to see myself much like a famous reggae star who'd just released a number one album, and now had to produce another hit. The fans were waiting (at least I thought they were). So each day at the library, I flipped through my books looking for that next big idea.

Many people who came to see my windmill kept saying the same thing:

"This looks like an antenna," or "If you can make this electric wind, you can make one of those. That's what it looks like anyway."

This made me curious how an antenna actually worked, and after thinking about it for a while, I went to Geoffrey with an idea.

"*Eh*, these people are always saying our windmill is an antenna, so let's give them what they want."

"What do you mean?"

"Let's build a radio station."

That afternoon, we rummaged through our bag of parts and found two junker radios that didn't even have covers attached. I wanted to test a theory. One night a few weeks before, there'd been a big thunderstorm. I was in my room listening to the Sunday Top Twenty when a huge crack of lightning exploded and caused a blip on my program, as if the lightning had sliced through my signal.

So taking the two radios, I tuned one to a static frequency, then took the second and tuned it to the same place on the dial. When this happened, the second radio went silent: no static, nothing. Was the frequency from one radio penetrating the other, just like the lightning bolt? If that was true, surely I could put my own voice on top of that frequency and let it ride into the next radio.

One of the radios I was using was a Walkman with both AM/FM and a cassette player. So leaving the first radio tuned to static, I took the Walkman and switched it to the tape mode. I noticed that wires ran from the tape head to the speakers, so I unhooked and reconnected them to the player's condenser, which controls the frequency. Perhaps music meant for the speakers could instead catch a ride on a frequency wave straight into its fellow radio.

I put my Black Missionaries tape in the deck.

"Here it goes," I said.

I pressed PLAY And sure enough, the music played loud and clear in the other radio! The Walkman was my transmitter, meaning that if I had five radios tuned to the same frequency, they'd all be playing the Black Missionaries.

"Now, Mister Geoffrey," I said, "how can I do this with my voice?"

I unhooked the wires from the condenser and reconnected them to a separate speaker, which I'd broken off a pair of headphones, turning it into a microphone. I pressed PLAY again and started talking into the mic.

"One two, one two," I said.

I could hear my voice coming from the other player.

"Good afternoon, Malawi. This is your host William Kamkwamba, along with my trusty sidekick, Mister Geoffrey. Your regularly scheduled program has been interrupted."

After that, Geoffrey and I began experimenting with our little radio station. Geoffrey walked outside with the radio, while I stayed in my room and started singing his favorite Billy Kaunda songs. Even outside, Geoffrey could hear my voice clearly. I held nothing back.

After a while he shouted, "My ears are bleeding! But please, carry on. This is cool!"

But the farther he got from my bedroom, the weaker the signal. After three hundred feet, it completely disappeared, which was probably good for Geoffrey, on account of my lousy voice.

"If we only had an amplifier, we could broadcast to greater distances," I said.

But Geoffrey was scared we'd be arrested for messing with the government's frequencies. People kept saying this same nonsense about my windmill: "You'd better be careful, or ESCOM will come and arrest you."

If the first people to experiment with great inventions such as radios, generators, or airplanes had been afraid of being arrested, we'd never be enjoying those things today.

"Let them come arrest me," I told them. "It would be an honor."

Soon I was attacking every idea with its own experiment.

Over the course of the next year, I was constantly planning or devising some new scheme. And while the windmill and radio station had been successful, I couldn't say the same for other ventures.

The project I was most excited about was a water pump—which had been part of my original idea that day in the library. Just as I'd done with my windmill, I first designed an experimental pump so I could play around with the concept. I modeled it after a picture in *Explaining Physics* of a standard force pump, which uses a piston and series of valves to push water through an outlet. The best example was the hand pumps my mother and sisters used in Wimbe to get our water.

My goal was to build a pump over the shallow well at our house. It was nothing but a forty-foot hole where we took water for washing clothes and floors. (It wasn't clean enough to drink.) The only way to get the water was by using a long rope and a bucket. To pump water, I'd need a pipe, and one that was long enough to reach the bottom of the well.

Just a few days earlier, I'd stumbled over some irrigation pipes buried in the ground at the scrapyard that I must have overlooked. Taking my hoe, I went one morning and dug them up.

The first was a wide PVC pipe, which I used as my outer barrel. I placed it down the well until I felt it hit the bottom. The second pipe was metal and slightly thinner, perfect for my piston. Mister Godsten then welded a round metal washer to the end of the pipe and left its center hole open. Around the washer I attached a thick piece of tire rubber that acted as the seal. I then had Godsten bend the top of the pipe to make a handle.

When the metal pipe was pushed up and down, it created a kind of vacuum inside the outer PVC pipe. When you pulled up, the water was sucked into the plastic pipe, and when you pushed down, the rubber seal opened and pushed the water to the surface, then out a small hole and into a bucket.

But the problem was, the rubber valve created too much friction against the plastic pipe. My mother and sisters tried using the pump, along with some other women, but they found it too difficult to operate.

"I can't manage this thing," my mother said. "It feels stuck."

I tried greasing the pipe, but the cold water made the grease too thick and clumpy. After a while, I gave it up.

The pump was a failure, but it was nothing compared to my attempt to create biogas.

As I mentioned earlier, deforestation in Malawi has made it difficult to find firewood for cooking, and gathering wood only adds to this destructive cycle. A good harvest of maize usually gave us enough dried cobs to burn for about four months. But once those were finished, the hunt for wood began.

In addition to fetching water in Wimbe, my mother and my sisters routinely walked two miles to the small blue-gum forest near Kachokolo to cut down a bundle of thin trees—a chore that took at least three hours. This wood was still green, and burning it produced thick white smoke that poured from our kitchen windows. Looking inside, I'd see my poor mother stirring the pot of *nsima*, squeezing her eyes closed as tears ran down her cheeks. All the girls in my family developed nasty coughs each year.

In Malawi, this is every woman's burden. And I knew these journeys to find wood would only get longer and longer. Plus, the deforestation would only create more devastating droughts and floods.

Someone had to save our women and trees, and I thought, *Why not me?*

Ever since I'd built the windmill, women asked me, "Does electric wind allow your mother to cook?" The answer was no. My windmill didn't supply enough voltage to power a hot plate, much less an electric stove or oven.

But a few weeks earlier, I was experimenting with wires and batteries and struck upon an idea. I took a long piece of copper wire and wrapped it twenty times around a thick piece of grass—the kind we used to build our roofs and fences. I connected both ends to a twelve-volt battery and felt it heat up. Soon the wire was glowing red-hot and the grass caught fire in my hands. It was a simple, kind of stupid experiment, but it really got me thinking: *Maybe something like this could boil water.*

I couldn't place a metal pot atop a coil of wire because it would act as a conductor. A clay pot was too heavy and would crush the coil. So I built a kind of magic wand using an empty ballpoint pen. These kinds of coils existed already—I'd seen them in the trading center—but they were powered by ESCOM electricity. I connected mine to a twelve-volt battery and dipped the coil into the water. In about five minutes, it was boiling.

But this was too simple. I had to go bigger. My *Integrated Science* book had a small section on alternative fuels, such as solar and hydro—both of which I'd studied. But it also mentioned something called biogas, which was made by converting animal poop into fuel to use for cooking. The book described a long process to get this gas—first you had to bury the poop in a pit, then wait months and months before the gas could be tapped with a valve. But I couldn't be bothered.

I don't need a pit, I thought. *And I certainly don't need to wait that long.*

So I devised my own plan. I snuck into my mother's kitchen and snatched the round clay pot she used for making beans. Now all I needed was the "organic matter," as the book described it, and I didn't have to look far. Across the compound, Aunt Chrissy kept two goats in a wooden pen behind her house, and the ground was covered with their marble-shaped poop. Taking a sugar bag, I made sure nobody was looking and climbed over the fence. I filled the sack until it was spilling over and walked back to the kitchen.

My mother was busy in the garden, which gave me plenty of time to work. First, I dumped the poop into the pot and filled it halfway with water, causing the brown, grassy balls to bob and float. I then covered the top of the pot with a plastic *jumbo* bag and tied a rope around the lip, sealing it tight. For my valve, I clipped the top off a radio antenna and poked the hollow tube through the center of the plastic. Lastly, I corked the top with a reed.

My mother's fire was still warm from breakfast, so I added a handful of maize cobs until the coals caught life. I placed the pot in the center and waited for greatness.

"Kamkwamba," I said to myself. "You've really done it this time."

In a few minutes, I heard a rumbling inside the pot as the water began to boil. The plastic puffed and danced from the steam, but the rope held tight. My heart began to flutter. I'd give it a few more seconds before initiating the final test.

That's when my mother came in.

"What's that smell?" she shouted.

I stammered, "B-biogas, it's—"

"It's horrible! What are you doing in here?"

I had no time to explain. By now the plastic was rumbling like mad, ready to blow. I had to act quickly. It was time to remove the reed and proceed with ignition.

I reached over and uncorked the valve, and when I did, a pipe of silver gas came rushing out the top. My mother

236

was right, it smelled terrible. I grabbed a long piece of grass that I'd set aside and poked it into the fire, catching a flame. I stood up and ran to the door, pushing my mother aside.

"Stand back!" I shouted. "This could be dangerous."

"*What?*"

With half my body protected by the doorframe, I thrust the flaming torch toward the valve and shielded my eyes from the blast. But when the fire touched the gas, all it did was fizzle and die. I was left holding a wet piece of grass, dripping with poopy water.

My mother was furious. She dragged me out of the kitchen, yelling, "Look what you've done, you've ruined my best cooking pot! Boiling goat poop! Wait until I tell your father!"

I tried to tell her I was doing it for her sake, but I guess it wasn't the right time.

In 2006, when I was eighteen years old, another famine struck Malawi.

That year, thanks to a change in government, my family had been able to buy a few bags of fertilizer. At first, the rains came like they normally do. We planted our seeds and waited for them to show their faces, then added a spoonful of fertilizer and a lot of prayer.

By January the seedlings were ankle high and showing their little arms, so happy to be drinking up such delicious rain. But just about the time they reached my father's knees, the rains stopped completely. By the time *dowe* season arrived, most of the ears were deformed. The government quickly promised help, but in the meantime, people grew angry and scared.

During the famine of 2001–02, people blamed the corrupt officials who'd sold off our surplus. But this time, instead of acknowledging the weather, they blamed magic. And that meant blaming me.

Superstitions were still very strong throughout the country, and several incidents in the news had stirred fears even more. During the previous famine, we heard lots of reports about vampires stealing people's body parts and selling them. Following the vampires, a strange beast appeared in Dowa and began attacking villages. Some said it looked like a hyena, others said it was a lion with the face of a dog. The attacks caused thousands to flee their homes and sleep in the forest, where they were even more vulnerable to this exotic creature.

The police conducted all-night searches. Then one evening, they managed to corner the beast in a thicket and opened fire with their rifles. But instead of falling dead, the beast split into three separate animals and disappeared into the bush. Villagers summoned their *sing'anga*, who concocted a powerful potion and flung it into the trees. The next morning, the beast lay dead on the road—its single corpse no bigger than a dog. Later it was discovered that the animal was the product of magic. A certain trader near Dowa had purchased some thunder and lightning from a powerful witch doctor and refused to pay for it. In retaliation, the wizard sent a monster against his village.

These stories, however ridiculous, only increased people's fears in evil powers. So in 2006, when it looked as if another famine was coming, people blamed magic. For weeks we'd gone without rain, then finally one day in March, giant storm clouds appeared in the distance. The sight of oily, black thunderheads was something to celebrate.

"Look," people said. "Today we'll have rain!"

"Finally we're saved!"

But as the clouds came overhead, a strong wind began to blow. It whipped the red dirt into our eyes and mouths and sent little cyclones tearing through the fields. Little by little, the storm drifted away without leaving a drop.

With nothing but the scorching sun left in the sky, people gathered at my house and pointed up to my windmill. The blades were spinning so fast, the tower rocked and swayed.

"Look, this giant fan has blown away the clouds. His machine is chasing away our rain!"

"This machine is evil!"

"It's not a machine—it's a witch tower. This boy is calling witches."

"Wait a second," I said. "The drought is all over the country. It's not just here, and electric wind is not the cause."

"But we saw it with our own eyes!" they said.

I was afraid these people would return one day and tear down my windmill, or worse. All the next week I stayed inside. I even stopped the blades during the day so they wouldn't raise more suspicions.

At the trading center, people approached Gilbert.

"You can tell us the truth," they said. "Is it true what he says about this electric wind? Or is he really a witch?"

"He isn't a witch," Gilbert answered. "It's a windmill, a scientific machine. I helped him build it."

"Are you sure?"

"I'm sure. You've seen it for yourself."

Many of them had even used my windmill to charge their mobile phones. But placing the blame on me helped them overcome their fears about the famine. Luckily, not long after that, the government stepped in and released tons of maize on the market. A few months later, some aid agencies arrived and offered more assistance. No one starved or died. A catastrophe had been avoided, but still, it underlined the kind of backwardness in our people that really frustrates me.

CHAPTER FOURTEEN
THE WORLD DISCOVERS WIMBE

Despite the incident with the famine, my popularity as an inventor led to other opportunities. That same year, one of the teachers at Wimbe Primary asked if I'd be interested in starting a science club for the students. He was impressed by my windmill and wanted one on campus.

"The students look up to you," he said. "Your skills in science will really challenge their brains."

"Sure," I said. "I'll do it."

The windmill I created for the school was small, much like my first radio experiment. For the blades, I used a metal maize pail, and the generator was a radio motor. I attached it to a blue-gum pole and ran the wires into my old Panasonic two-battery radio. I did this during recess one morning when all the kids were playing soccer. When I connected the wires, and music blasted through the schoolyard, a small riot erupted from all the excitement.

The windmill not only allowed students to listen to music and news, but they could also charge their parents' mobile phones. Each Monday, I explained to them the basics of science and gave some popular examples of simple innovation, like how ink was first made by using charcoal. I also demonstrated the cup-and-string experiment featured in my books, to help explain how a telephone works.

I walked them through the steps of how I'd built everything using everyday materials.

"So many things around you are reusable," I told them. "Where others see garbage, I see opportunity."

I hoped I was inspiring them in some way, because if I could teach my neighbors how to build windmills, I thought, what else could we build together?

"In science we invent and create," I continued. "We make new things that can benefit our situation. If we can all invent something to make our lives better, we can change Malawi."

I later found out that some of the students had been so inspired by the windmill, they'd gone home and made toy versions themselves.

I imagined what it would be like if all those pinwheels were real. What if every home and shop in Wimbe had machines on the rooftops to catch the wind? At night, the entire valley would sparkle like a clear sky full of stars. Bringing electricity to my people no longer seemed like a madman's dream.

In early November 2006, some officials from the Malawi Teacher Training Activity were inspecting the library at Wimbe Primary when they noticed my windmill in the schoolyard. They asked Ms. Sikelo who'd built it and she gave them my name. One of them telephoned his boss, Dr. Hartford Mchazime, and described what he'd seen.

A few days later, Dr. Mchazime drove five hours to Wimbe. He was even more amazed once he saw the larger windmill at my house, and he asked my father if he could speak with the boy who'd built it.

"He's here," my father said, and called me from my room.

Dr. Mchazime was an older man with gray hair and kind, patient eyes. But when he spoke, his command of language was large and powerful. I'd never heard anyone speak such good Chichewa, and when he spoke English, it was simply eloquent.

He asked me about the windmill and how it came about. "Tell me everything," he said.

I told the story as I'd done a hundred times before, then took him through the house demonstrating how my switches and the circuit breaker worked. He listened carefully, nodding his head, and asked specific questions.

"These are very tiny bulbs. Why aren't you using big ones?"

"I can use big ones," I said, "but big lights require more voltage. The dynamo is only so strong."

"How far did you go with your education?"

"Just the first year in secondary school."

"Then how did you know this stuff about voltage and power?"

"I've been borrowing books from your library."

"Who teaches you this stuff? Who helps you?"

"No one," I said. "I've been reading and doing it alone."

Dr. Mchazime then went to see my parents.

"You have lights in your house because of your son," he said. "What do you think of this?"

"We thought he was mad," my mother said.

Dr. Mchazime laughed and shook his head.

"I want to tell you something," he said. "You may not realize, but your son has done an amazing thing, and this is only the beginning. You're going to see a lot more people coming here to see William Kamkwamba. I have a feeling this boy will go far. I want you to be ready."

The visit left me a little confused and very excited. No one had ever asked me such questions before, and no one had taken that kind of interest. That afternoon, Dr. Mchazime returned to his office in Zomba and told his colleagues what he'd seen.

"This is fantastic," they said. "The whole world needs to know about this boy."

"I agree," said Dr. Mchazime. "And I have just the idea."

The next week, Dr. Mchazime returned to my house with a journalist from Radio One. It was the famous Everson Maseya, whose voice I'd heard for years. He'd come to my house to interview *me*.

"What do you call this thing?" he asked.

"I'm calling it electric wind."

"But how does it work?"

"The blades spin and generate power from a dynamo."

"And in the future, what do you want to do with this?"

"I want to reach every village in Malawi so people can have lights and water."

While we waited for the Radio One interview to air, Dr. Mchazime came with even more reporters. These men represented all the great media organizations in Malawi: Mudziwithu and Zodiak Radio channels, *The Daily Times*, the *Nation*, and *Malawi News*. They poured out of the car with their cameras and tape recorders, and flocked around the windmill.

For two hours, they moved through the house, elbowing and shoving one another to get the best pictures of my switches and battery system.

"You've had your time. Now it's my turn!"

"Move aside, my paper is bigger!"

Soon our yard was filled with crowds from the trading center who'd come to gawk at the famous journalists.

"Look, it's Noel Mkubwi from Zodiak!" they said.

"Finally we see his face. What a handsome man!"

"And he's interviewing William!"

One of the reporters even climbed my tower and studied the blades and chain system, taking pictures the whole time.

"Mchazime, this chap is a genius," he shouted.

"Yes," he answered, "and this is the problem with our

system. We're losing talent like this all the time as a result of poverty. And when we do send them back to school, it's not a good education. I'm bringing you here because I want the world to see what this boy has done, and I want them to help."

Like me, Dr. Mchazime's father had also been a poor farmer who struggled to feed and clothe his family. But he knew the value of an education.

At one point when Dr. Mchazime was young, he had volunteered to drop out of school and work so his brothers could go instead. His father refused, saying, "All of my kids will stay in school. I'll do whatever it takes." It took nearly ten years for Dr. Mchazime to complete his secondary education. He later earned degrees from universities in Malawi, America, Britain, and South Africa. Before working for the MTTA, he'd written many Malawian textbooks, including my own Standard Eight English reader.

The day after the journalists came to visit, the interview finally aired on Radio One. I was behind the house chatting with my aunt, when my mother shouted, "William, quick. It's coming on!"

My family gathered around the radio and I heard the

announcer say, "A boy in Wimbe near Kasungu has made electric wind." When my voice came through the speakers, my sisters began to cheer.

If the radio show weren't enough good fortune, the story in the *Daily Times* was published the following week, with a big headline that said: "School Dropout with a Streak of Genius." The story had a photo of me pretending to connect the wires to the battery in my room, still unable to wipe the smile from my face. That afternoon, I took the paper to the trading center to show everyone what the madman had done.

"We also heard you on the radio," they said. "We're so impressed at how well you spoke."

In a way, it took having these reporters come to my house to make our town finally accept my windmill. After the media coverage, the number of visitors to my house increased tenfold.

Shortly after, I started some much-needed improvements on the windmill. I realized the big mango tree behind the latrine was blocking my strongest wind and I needed to go higher. My father, with the *Daily Times* story under his arm, was able to convince the manager of the tobacco estate to give me several giant poles, which I used to build a tower that was thirty-six feet high. Once

I moved it away from the mango tree, the speed of my blades doubled, and so did the voltage.

The day after the *Daily Times* article ran, a Malawian in Lilongwe named Soyapi Mumba brought the article to his office. Soyapi worked as a software engineer and coder at Baobab Health Partnership, an American charity organization that was working to computerize Malawi's health care system. One of Soyapi's colleagues, a tall American named Mike McKay, liked the article about my windmill so much that he wrote about me on his blog, *Hacktivate*. That blog entry caught the attention of Emeka Okafor, a famous Nigerian author and blogger, who is also the program director of something called the TED Global Conference.

Well, Emeka wanted me to apply to be an official "fellow" at this conference, and for three weeks, tried very hard to find me. After harassing the reporters at the paper every day, he finally tracked down Dr. Mchazime.

In mid-December 2006, Dr. Mchazime came to my home with the application and paperwork for TED. We sat down under the mango tree, and he helped me answer a list of questions, plus write a small essay about my life. When he left, I still had no idea what TED was, though I do now: It means Technology, Entertainment, and Design, and it's an annual meeting where scientists and innovators get together and share their big ideas.

I wasn't entirely sure what a *conference* was, or what people did at such things. The application didn't even say where it was held. I suspected Lilongwe, the capital, but didn't know. I imagined myself walking those busy streets and seeing all sorts of new people. I wondered what clothes I would need to wear, since everything I owned hung from a rope in my bedroom and was covered in red roof dust. Even still, it gave me something to dream about.

The following week, Dr. Mchazime called to say that TED had chosen me. The conference would be held in Arusha, Tanzania—an entirely different country.

"You'll be honored with other scientists and inventors," he said. "People from all over the world will be there. Perhaps something good can come from it."

Wow, Arusha. How long would that bus ride take, and what if I got hungry? I'd have to bring plenty of food, perhaps cakes and roasted maize. After all, I had no money.

"One important thing," he said. "We should book your flight before it fills up."

"I'm traveling by plane? *My God*."

251

"Yes, and they wish to know if you want a smoking or non-smoking room in the hotel."

"I'm staying at a hotel?" I thought for sure I'd be sleeping in one of those guesthouses near the boozing dens where poor people stay.

"Of course you're staying in a hotel," he said. "And I have other good news. William, you're going back to school."

After visiting my house with the reporters, Dr. Mchazime approached the government about accepting me into a school. He'd even taken a collection among his colleagues to help pay for my first semester.

The process had taken months. Finally, the Ministry of Education had granted me permission to attend Madisi Secondary, a public boarding school an hour from my home. It wasn't one of the science-based schools I'd longed to attend. The headmasters at those places weren't willing to accept me on account of my old age and number of years I'd been a dropout.

However, the headmaster of Madisi, Mister Rhonex Banda, was so moved by my story that he offered to spend the extra time with me, helping me catch up. I was terribly behind.

While Dr. Mchazime planned my trip to Arusha, I

packed my things and went to school. This was the first time I'd ever lived away from home. In my suitcase I packed a toothbrush and toothpaste, flip-flops, a blanket, and all my dirt-streaked clothes. I carried it out through the courtyard and stopped under the mango tree, where Geoffrey and my parents were waiting.

"I guess I'll see you soon," I told them.

"Work hard," my father said. "I want you to know we're very proud."

Geoffrey strapped my suitcase to his bicycle, and we rolled it toward the truck stop. Along the way, I said good-bye to Gilbert.

"We don't have phones, so how will we talk?" he asked.

"It will be difficult," I said.

"Maybe I can come visit you there."

"Oh, Gilbert, that would be great. Please do."

"I'll miss you, friend."

"For sure."

A pickup soon appeared in a cloud of dust. Geoffrey waved his hand and flagged down the driver.

"I'll see you when school ends," he said. "When you arrive, find someone with a phone and send me their number. We'll talk this way, and I'll make sure Gilbert is there."

"That would be good," I said. "Take care of my windmill, will you? Let me know everything that happens."

"Sure, sure, don't worry."

I climbed aboard with the other passengers, found a sack of charcoal for a seat, and we rolled toward Kasungu. Once there, I caught a minibus down the M1 highway to the small town of Madisi. The minibus dropped me at a junction on the outskirts of town, where a long road led to the school. I walked a kilometer with my suitcase bouncing behind on the gravel road, until I stood outside the gates. In a matter of minutes, I had a dorm room and dorm mates, meal times, and a rigorous schedule of classes. Everything was new and foreign and a little overwhelming—but my God, what a pleasure it was to be learning in a real school.

The classrooms in Madisi had solid roofs that didn't leak, and smooth, unblemished concrete floors. Large windows let in the sunshine, but kept out the cold. I had an actual desk of my own, complete with pencil holder. During study sessions at night, real fluorescent lights buzzed overhead, or at least they did when there wasn't a blackout.

Science class was held in an actual chemistry lab, where the shelves were lined with microscopes, giant coils of high-resistance wire, glass beakers, and old jars of boric acid. If you can believe it, one of the first lessons in science class was how current passes through an electric bell. I'd already applied this concept with my windmill and circuit breaker, but having it explained in scientific terms—and in English—was like hearing it for the first time.

But like every other school in Malawi, Madisi relied on the government to survive. Unlike some of the more prestigious boarding schools, it had been forgotten. Most of the equipment in the science lab was old and no longer worked. The chemicals had expired and were dangerous, the microscopes were rusted and scratched. For the electric bell lecture, we had no batteries to supply the power.

"If anyone has an extra one in their rooms, I'm happy to demonstrate," the teacher said.

No one did, so we used our imaginations.

Our dorms were also dirty, and the walls were covered with graffiti. The urinals in the bathroom didn't work, so the new students (namely me) had to clean them every day to keep down the smell. The rooms themselves were so cramped that we each had to share our bed with another boy. My bedmate was a guy named Kennedy, who never cleaned his socks.

"*Eh*, man, you need to wash your feet before you come to bed with me," I told him.

"Sorry, I can't ever tell," he said. "I'll wash tomorrow, promise."

But he never did. Often I'd wake up with his feet touching my mouth.

And because I was years older than everyone else, some of the students teased me.

They shouted, "How many kids did you leave behind at the farm, old man?"

"Two boys," I said, "and one more on the way. Perhaps next month."

"He thinks he's funny," they said. "He's spending too much time with his cows."

One day I decided to end the teasing once and for all. I pulled out the newspaper article about my windmill and slapped it down on the table.

"Here," I said. "This is what I was doing."

My dorm mates were impressed. "Good job, man!" they said.

No one teased me after that.

Honestly, it really didn't bother me. Because after five years of being a dropout, I was grateful to be in school. However, I did become homesick, and whenever that happened, I'd hide away in the school library, where the books filled rows and rows of shelves. I'd find a chair and study my lesson books in geography, social studies, biology, and math. I'd lose myself in American and African history, and within the colorful maps of the world. No matter how foreign and lonely the world was outside, the books always reminded me of home, sitting under the mango tree.

While I attended school at Madisi, Dr. Mchazime was busy making arrangements for Arusha. He helped me get a passport and even took a collection for a new white shirt and black trousers. They were the nicest clothes I'd ever owned. He also gave me useful travel advice: For instance, on a plane, I'd be assigned a seat that was mine and mine only. There was no need to rush and use your elbows like people did on Malawian buses. Also, if the red light was on near the bathroom, that meant it was occupied; and because some passengers become nauseous on their first plane ride, each seat came with a paper bag for vomit. This was good information, because I was certain I'd need it.

In June, I left school and came home to pack. The next morning, a driver appeared to take me to the airport in Lilongwe.

"Our son is leaving us and traveling by airplane," my father told my mother, smiling.

"That's right," I said. "Flying like a bird in the sky. I'll be waving as I pass over."

"We'll be watching for you. You'll see us here."

My father then tucked a bag of roasted peanuts in my pocket. They were still warm.

That evening, I was so nervous, I stayed awake in my hotel room watching soccer on Super Sport 3 until the sun came up and it was time to leave.

On the plane, I couldn't believe it, but sitting next to me was none other than Soyapi Mumba, the software engineer from Lilongwe who'd first seen my article. Because he's a nice guy, he introduced himself, not knowing who I was. When I told him my name and where I was going, he replied, "Oh my God, William the windmill guy?" He explained how excited he was to show the story to Mike McKay, who'd blogged about me on *Hacktivate*. Soyapi was the very reason anybody had ever heard about me, and now here he was, sitting next to me on the plane! It also happened that Soyapi was a TED fellow himself, being honored for his coding work with Baobab. I was so fortunate to find him.

As the plane taxied toward the runway, I began to notice the others seated around me. They looked so well-dressed and confident, like they had important things to do, and their busy lives required them to travel in jets across the world. As the plane accelerated and lifted its nose in the air, I pressed my head back against the seat and laughed.

I was now one of them too.

CHAPTER FIFTEEN
MEETING TED AND TOM

After arriving in Arusha, I boarded a bus to the Ngurdoto Mountain Lodge, where the conference was being held. As the bus exited the airport, I gazed out the window to see if Tanzania looked any different from Malawi, but what I saw was very similar: The highway was filled with minibuses crammed with people; a giant lorry belched smoke and swerved to miss an old man on a bicycle. There were children in rags hawking cigarettes on the roadside, while students in bright uniforms marched through the dust to school. I saw village women balancing loads of vegetables on their heads and farmers tending their fields.

But unlike Malawi, Arusha had trees—and not only that. After some minutes, the shuttle driver pointed off in the distance and said, "Look there—Kilimanjaro. Biggest mountain in Africa."

Mount Kilimanjaro appeared even more grand and majestic than I'd seen in books, with ribbons of white snow along its peak and cloaked in a thin layer of clouds. It was hard to imagine that ordinary people like myself actually climbed to the top, but I knew they did. In my head, I began making a list of all the other places in the world I wanted to see.

That mountain filled me with great confidence, but it all seemed to vanish once I reached the hotel. The lobby was a scene of chaos and confusion, filled with white people speaking English and Africans with strange and foreign accents. Everyone was chatting on their mobile phones and talking in loud, booming voices. I prayed that no one would speak to me, and after registering at the welcome center, I walked to the corner of the room and tried to disappear.

No such luck. After some minutes, a man walked up

and stuck out his hand. He had red hair and wore purple-and-green eyeglasses.

"Hello, welcome to TED," he said. "My name is Tom. Who are you?"

I'd practiced only one line of English, so I let it fly: "I'm William Kamkwamba, and I'm from Malawi."

He stared at me strangely. Maybe I'd said it in Chichewa.

"Wait a minute," he said. "You're the guy with the windmill."

Tom Rielly was in charge of organizing all the corporate sponsors at TED, including the ones who'd paid for my airfare and hotel. Months earlier in New York, Emeka—the Nigerian blogger—had told Tom about my windmill, saying, "You'll never believe this story . . ." But Tom didn't know that Emeka had then searched under every rock in Malawi to find me.

After talking a while, Tom asked if I wanted to tell my story on stage—in front of all these people.

I shrugged. *Why not?*

"Do you have a computer?" he asked.

I shook my head.

"Do you have any photos of the windmill?"

I did have these. A friend of Dr. Mchazime's had visited Madisi a few weeks earlier and helped prepare a presentation in case I needed it. He'd done this on his laptop—though at the time I had no idea this was a computer. To me, computers were big like televisions and plugged into the wall.

Before the man left, he handed me a strange cube—a flash drive—attached to a rope and said, "Wear this around your neck. This is your presentation."

So when Tom asked about my photos, I handed him the cube. He then plugged it into another laptop and said, "I'll just copy these onto my computer."

It was then I realized what a laptop was. *Of course,* I thought. *It's a portable computer. What a good idea!*

Sensing my delight at this discovery, Tom asked me, "William, have you ever seen the Internet?"

The what? "No," I said.

In a quiet conference room, Tom sat me down and introduced me to this most amazing tool.

"This is Google," he said. "You can find answers to anything. What do you want to search for?"

That was easy. "Windmill."

In one second, he pulled up five million page results—pictures and models of windmills I'd never even imagined.

My God, I thought, *where was this Google when I needed it?*

Next, we pulled up a map of Malawi, then a photo of

Wimbe itself, taken from a camera in outer space.

It's funny to me now—at this conference in East Africa, with some of the world's greatest innovators of science and technology just outside the door, there I was in this room seeing the Internet for the first time.

Tom helped me set up my own e-mail account, and for the next week, he introduced me to a range of technology: smartphones, video and 35mm cameras, even an iPod Nano, which I turned over and over in my hand before finally asking, "Where is the battery?" (Not long after, I'd be hacking into iPods and iPhones and repairing them for people.)

But the most amazing thing about TED wasn't the Internet, the gadgets, or even the breakfast buffets with three kinds of meat, plus eggs and pastries and fruits that I dreamt about each night. It was the other Africans who stood on stage and shared their visions of how to make our continent a better place.

There was Corneille Ewango, a biologist from Congo who'd risked his life to save endangered animals during the country's civil war; he'd even buried his Land Rover engines and stashed lab equipment in the trees to hide them from the rebels. A man from Ethiopia invented a kind of refrigerator that works using water evaporation from sand. Others were doctors and scientists using creative ideas and methods to fight AIDS, malaria, and tuberculosis. Even Erik Hersman was there—one of the first people, along with Mike McKay, to write about my windmill on his blog *Afrigadget*. Erik was raised in Kenya and Sudan as the son of missionaries. What he said summed up our crowd perfectly:

"Where the world sees trash, Africa recycles. Where the world sees junk, Africa sees rebirth."

As far as my presentation went—when I heard Chris Anderson, the event's host, call my name, my legs refused to work.

"Don't worry," Tom whispered, squeezing my shoulder. "Just take a deep breath."

My heart beat fast like a *mganda* drum as I climbed the steps to face the audience, which totaled about four hundred fifty people—all the inventors and scientists and doctors who'd shared their stories and ideas the previous days. They were now watching me. When I reached the stage and turned around, I went completely blind. Lights from the ceiling were shining into my eyes, so bright I couldn't even think. All the words I'd prepared seemed to dance to the drum and get lost in the glare.

"We've got a picture," said Chris. He pointed to something behind me, and a giant photo of my parents' house appeared. I saw the mud-brick walls, grass roof, bright blue sky. I could feel the sun.

"Where is this?" he asked.

"This is my home. This is where I live."

"Where? What country?"

"In Malawi Kasungu," I said, then quickly corrected myself. "Ah, Kasungu, Malawi." My hands began to shake.

"Five years ago you had an idea," Chris said. "What was that?"

"I want to made a windmill."

Chris smiled. "So what did you do, how did you realize that?"

I took a deep breath and gave it my best. "After I drop out from school, I went to library, and I get information about windmill . . ."

Keep going, keep going . . .

"And I try, and I made it."

I expected the audience to laugh at my silly English, but to my surprise, all I heard was applause. Not only were they clapping, but they were standing and cheering. And when I finally returned to my seat, I noticed that several were even crying.

After all the years of trouble—the famine and fear for

my family, dropping out of school, Khamba's death, and the teasing I received trying to develop my idea—I was finally being recognized. For the first time in my life, I felt I was surrounded by people who understood what I did. A huge weight seemed to leave my chest and fall to the assembly hall floor. I could finally relax. I was now among colleagues.

For the next couple of days, they lined up to meet me.

"William, can I take my photo with you?"

"William, please join us for lunch!"

One line from my presentation even became a kind of motto for the conference. Everywhere I went, people shouted, "I try, and I made it!" I was so flattered. I wished my parents, Gilbert, and Geoffrey had been there to see it. They would have been proud.

When I first met Tom, he asked what I hoped to obtain someday in my life. I told him I had two goals: to remain in school and to build a bigger windmill to irrigate my family's crops, so we'd never go hungry again.

Basically, this was *every* Malawians' wish. But Tom seemed confident, and over the next several days, he approached many of his friends and colleagues at the conference and asked for their help. By the time it was over, he'd raised enough money to get me started. I'm so grateful to everyone who assisted me and I pray that God blesses them all.

After the conference, Tom flew back to Malawi to meet my family and to help enroll me in a better school. When the taxi turned onto the dirt road toward my house, the windmill appeared in the distance, looking so beautiful. As usual, its blades were spinning fast and causing the tower to sway back and forth.

"It's more than functional," Tom said. "William, this is art."

I gave him a tour of the compound, showing him the car battery and bulb. He laughed at the pile of radio and tractor parts in the corner of my room.

"I think every great inventor has a pile of junk some-place," he said.

I also demonstrated the light switches, circuit breaker, and the way I'd waterproofed my bulb outside. For the porch light, all I had were Christmas lights, so I hollowed out a regular incandescent bulb and wired the Christmas lights inside. This shell served as both a weather protector and diffuser.

"There's more to this than I thought," Tom said.

I just laughed. I hadn't even told him about the famine.

Back in Lilongwe, Tom and I visited the offices of Baobab Health, located on the grounds of Kamuzu Central Hospital, to see Soyapi and finally meet Mike McKay. Baobab was founded in 2000 by a British-American computer scientist named Gerry Douglas, who'd invented a new kind of software to help Malawi hospitals register and treat patients more effectively.

Gerry was out of town at the time of our visit, so Mike and Soyapi gave us the tour. Mike started by showing me a small windmill kit they were hoping to use to power a village clinic. Its generator was a treadmill motor, which I'd never seen. He stuck a power drill in one end of the motor to make it spin, then took the two wires and attached them to a voltmeter—an amazing gadget! The voltmeter measured the motor's power at forty-eight volts, which was four times stronger than my dynamo.

"What do you think?" Mike asked.

"*Yah*, it's cool."

He then gave them both to me as a gift.

"Oh, thank you!" I said. The hole in heaven just kept getting wider.

Mike and Soyapi also introduced me to deep-cycle batteries. Compared to my car battery, they provide a more stable amount of current for longer periods of time. I wanted to try one of these, so Tom and I went to the offices of Solair, a local solar-power dealer. We bought two batteries and four solar lamps, along with energy-saving bulbs and materials to rewire my entire compound.

Workers arrived at my village the following week, and for three days, we replaced old wiring, dug trenches to bury cables, and installed proper light fixtures and plugs (though I kept my old flip-flop switches just for fun).

With quality wire, a plastic conduit, and buried lines, we never had to worry about fires again. I also stuck a lightning rod on top of the windmill just in case. Once it was finished, there was a bulb for every room, including two outside.

I also installed solar panels on my roof to help store electricity when the wind wasn't blowing. These days, every home in my village has one of these panels, complete with a battery to store power.

With each home lighted, the compound finally glowed at night.

After being refused by several schools because of my age, I was finally accepted at African Bible College and Christian Academy (ABCCA) in Lilongwe, which was run by Presbyterian missionaries. The headmaster, Chuck Wilson, was an American from California, and my teacher, Lorilee Maclean, was from Canada.

Although I was behind the other students, Mrs. Maclean and Mister Wilson agreed to take a chance on admitting me. But Mrs. Maclean had one condition: that when I left school each day, I didn't go home to poverty.

I had to find a place to live in Lilongwe.

Since I had no relatives in town, Gerry offered me a room at his house. I had my own bed and a desk for studying, and the housekeeper Nancy prepared plenty of *nsima* and relish so I didn't feel homesick. Everything was great, but because we were in the city, we experienced power cuts several times a week. After all that hardship to bring electricity to my village, here I was sitting in the dark in my success.

"You should carry a windmill everywhere you go," Gerry joked.

Over time, Gerry became a great friend and teacher. When he still lived in England, he flew airplanes and worked as a helicopter mechanic, so I always asked him questions about motors and such. Sometimes after dinner, he explained how helicopters worked, how the spinning blades captured wind to lift the heavy machines, and how the back rotors kept them from spinning in circles.

Gerry also helped me with my English, particularly my *L*'s and *R*'s—something we Chichewa speakers always get confused. These lessons were sometimes done in front of the bathroom mirror, so Gerry could demonstrate.

"Okay, William, watch my tongue and say 'library.'"

"Liblaly."

"Li-brrarry."

"Li-blaly."

"You'll get it."

My class at ABCCA used a distance-learning curriculum from America that we learned by computer over the Internet. Just a couple months before, I'd never even seen the Web, and now I used it every day to speak with teachers in Colorado.

At first, I was ashamed of my poor English, especially after hearing five-year-old children speak better sentences. During my first few days, I became quite depressed. But my tutor, a Malawian named Blessings Chikakula, offered some great encouragement.

Mister Blessings had also come from a poor village near Dowa, so poor that he was thirty years old before he got a college degree. Now he was working at ABCCA as a teacher.

"Don't be discouraged and give up just because it's

hard," Mister Blessings told me. "Whatever you want to do, if you do it with all your heart, it will happen."

Eventually, the money from my donors at TED allowed me to help my family in many other ways. I installed iron sheets on our compound to replace the grass roofs. I bought mattresses so my sisters didn't have to sleep on the dirt floor, plus covered water buckets to protect our drinking supply from pests; I bought better blankets to keep us warm at night in winter; malaria pills and mosquito nets for the rainy season; and I arranged to send everyone in my family to the doctor and dentist.

And for once, I finally managed to repay Gilbert for all the help he'd given me. Several years before, Gilbert's father had died, and he'd had to drop out of school for lack of money. So with my donations, I put Gilbert back in school, along with Geoffrey and several other cousins who'd dropped out during the famine. I even paid the neighbors' kids' tuition.

And after years of dreaming about it, I was finally able to drill a borehole for a deep well, which gave my family clean drinking water. My mother said this saved her two hours each day carrying water from the public well. Using a solar-powered pump, I filled two giant tanks and piped water to my father's field.

Irrigation allowed us to plant a second maize crop. The storage room would never be empty again. The spigot from the borehole was also free for all the women in Wimbe to use. It's the only running water for miles around, and each day, dozens of women come to my home to fill their buckets with clean, cool water without having to pump and pump.

During my holidays from school, I constructed a bigger windmill that pumped water, which I called the Green Machine on account of its color. That pump now sits above the shallow well at home and irrigates a garden where my mother grows spinach, carrots, tomatoes, and potatoes, both for my family to eat and to sell at market.

Finally, the dream had been accomplished.

My family couldn't have imagined that the little windmill I built during the famine would change their lives in every way, and they saw this change as a gift from heaven. Whenever I came home on weekends, my parents had a new nickname. They called me Noah—like the man in the Bible who built the ark, saving his family from God's flood.

"Everyone laughed at Noah, but look what happened," my mother said.

My father agreed. "You've put us on the map. Now the world knows we're here."

✳

In December 2007, I went to the United States to see the windmills of California, just like the ones in my textbook back home. I landed in New York City right in the middle of winter, wearing only a sweater. The woman at the airline counter then informed me they'd lost all my luggage.

"We'll call you," she said.

Huh? I didn't even have a phone.

Some of Tom's friends met me at the airport. As the taxi pulled out, I finally saw the great American city I'd read so much about. We drove over smooth roads with several lanes in each direction, across bridges with no water underneath, followed by more roads and more bridges. The tall buildings in the distance appeared so pressed together that it was hard to imagine people walking between them, much less building them.

It just so happened that Tom lived in one of those buildings in Lower Manhattan. His apartment was on the thirty-sixth floor, and I wondered how we would ever get up there. One of his friends then showed me the elevator.

"What is that?" I asked.

I pushed the button, and in ten seconds I was thirty-six floors up in the sky. Already, I had so many questions.

Inside, Tom greeted me heartily. His apartment was surrounded by windows, looking as if you could walk right over the edge. Before that day, the highest I'd ever been besides an airplane was the top of my windmill. It took some time to adjust, and that night, I had trouble sleeping.

The next day, I went underground into the subway, where I watched people enter the gates using sliding money cards—another great idea. The sidewalks of New York left me exhausted, with hundreds of people running in every direction. One of the things I noticed in New York is that people don't have time for anything, not even to sit down for coffee—instead, they drink it from paper cups while they walk and send text messages. Sometimes they walk right into you.

Touring the city, I began to wonder how Americans could build a skyscraper in a year, but in four decades of independence, Malawi couldn't even bring clean water to a village. We could send witch planes into the skies and ghost trucks along the roads, but we couldn't even keep electricity in our homes. We always seemed to be struggling to catch up. Even with so many smart and hardworking people, we were still living and dying like our ancestors.

The following week, I flew to California and visited the San Diego Wild Animal Park—where I saw giraffes, hippos, and elephants for the first time. You know, just a half hour from my home in Wimbe was the Kasungu National Park, where all of these same animals lived in the wild. But it took me flying ten thousand miles to America to finally see them up close. I had to laugh.

But of all the places I went, nothing impressed me more than the windmills of Palm Springs.

For a moment after entering the "wind farm," I felt like I was back home. The setting was familiar: lush green flatland and mountains in the distance, and all of it draped in a bright blue sky. But here, in that empty space between me and the hills, were miles upon miles of windmills. More than six thousand of them, shooting from the ground like giant mechanical trees.

The round white trunks were like cartoons I'd seen on television, so big around they could fit my family's entire house. Looking up, I saw the hundred-foot blades twirling slowly like the toys of God. Each one stood two hundred feet in the air, with a wingspan longer than the airplane that had brought me to America. The head engineer of the farm took me inside one of the machines, where computer screens revealed all kinds of information—everything from voltage output to wind and blade speed.

In total, the wind farm produced more than six thousand megawatts, which was delivered to thousands of homes by underground cable. By comparison, just six *hundred* megawatts could light up all of Malawi, with energy to spare. At the time, ESCOM produced only 224 megawatts.

It was an incredible feeling to see the machines that I'd imagined for so long. Now here they were, twisting in the wind before me. I realized I'd come full circle. The pictures in the book had provided the idea, hunger and darkness gave me inspiration, and I'd embarked myself on this long and amazing journey. Standing there, I waited for direction. What would I do next? What was in my future? Looking across the field of windmills, I saw how the mountains seemed to tumble and dance along their twirling blades.

They seemed to be telling me something—that I didn't have to decide right away. I could return to Africa and go back to school. After that, who knows? Perhaps I would study these machines and learn how to build them, then plant my own forest of mechanical trees in Malawi. Perhaps I could even teach people how to build simpler devices like I had at home so they could provide their own light and water. Perhaps I'd do both. Whatever I decided to do, this lesson would always stay with me:

If you want to make it, all you have to do is try.

EPILOGUE

While I was traveling in America over Christmas in 2007, I received some wonderful news. I'd been offered a scholarship to the African Leadership Academy (ALA), an exciting new high school that was opening in Johannesburg, South Africa. Its students were chosen from across Africa's fifty-three countries, with the goal to train the continent's next generation of leaders. Out of the 1,700 students who applied, only 106 were selected. Many were entrepreneurs and inventors like me who'd overcome hardships and were improving the lives of their families and neighbors. Others were simply the smartest kids in their countries, having scored the highest grades on their national exams.

In August, I went home to pack my bags and say good-bye once again to my family. The next morning, I boarded a plane for Johannesburg and began the next chapter of my life. Even though I'd worked extremely hard at my school in Lilongwe, I was still behind in English and math. The classes at ALA were just as difficult as I'd imagined, and for the first year I struggled. During times when my confidence sank low, I would daydream about my village and its simple comforts. I was terribly homesick.

But gradually, I improved. And as my spirits lifted, I began to realize what an amazing place I'd found. The school campus was beautiful—with giant shade trees, lush green soccer fields, and peacocks that strutted across the lawn. But the best part of ALA was the many friends I met, people who, despite their young age, had already led extraordinary lives.

There was Miranda Nyathi from KwaZakhele, South Africa. During a big teachers' strike that closed down her school, she began teaching the students herself—leading courses in math, science, and geography so no one's education would be interrupted. My friend Paul Lorem was a "Lost Boy" in Sudan who survived the country's civil war and lived without parents in a refugee camp. The same with my schoolmate Joseph Munyambanza, who escaped fighting in Congo and lived in a camp in Uganda, where he attended school in a tent.

For the first time in my life, I was surrounded by people

from a variety of backgrounds and cultures, and many of them speaking their own languages. I learned Swahili by chatting with my Kenyan roommate, Githiora, and my other friends from Kenya and Tanzania. My pals from Zimbabwe taught me Shona, and I even learned some Arabic from our Moroccan students.

Along with taking classes in leadership and entrepreneurship (which I loved), we were also required to volunteer in our surrounding community. My classmates and I helped a local orphanage by tending their garden. The vegetables were used to feed the children and to sell in the markets so they could buy clothing and other items. I was particularly good at this project because, in addition to being an inventor, I was first a farmer.

Graduation day was one I'll never forget. For the first time ever, my parents boarded an airplane and left Malawi. When they landed in Johannesburg—with its bright lights, commotion, and people speaking foreign languages—I didn't know if they would be happy or run terrified back to the plane. It helped that Geoffrey and Mister Blessings also came along to provide support and share the adventure. After a while, they were all laughing and marveling at this modern African city.

On graduation day, my father looked so proud. The minute he saw me in my cap and gown, his chest puffed out and a smile spread across his face. He called my mother over.

"Look at our son. Despite all of our troubles, the boy has done it."

"Yes," she said. "William, today you're making your parents very happy."

While all of this was going on, I was also working on the book about my life. My friend Bryan Mealer, a journalist who'd worked in Africa, came to live with me in my village for several months. He and Blessings spent their days interviewing me and my relatives, along with everyone in Wimbe who knew anything about me. At the end of each day, we sat down together and put all the stories to paper. Even after everything I'd been through, writing a book felt like an amazing accomplishment.

The Boy Who Harnessed the Wind was first published in September 2009. To help spread my story, Bryan and I embarked on our own adventure across America—one that included a dozen cities and fifteen different airplane rides. We spoke at schools, lecture halls, bookstores, and even appeared on the radio and television. In every city we visited, I was so encouraged by the large numbers of young people who showed up at our events.

Most were around the same age I was when I made my windmill, and some were even younger. The parents who brought them usually said something like, "The next time Billy complains about such and such, I'll tell him that William nearly starved!" This made me laugh, but really, the kids told me they enjoyed the book because it made science seem cool. It also made the world seem more interesting than anything they'd ever seen on television. I was really happy to hear such things. You know, if someone like me had ever visited Kachokolo when I was a student and talked about science and experiments, I would have never left him alone.

Toward the end of my book tour, I was lucky enough to visit Dartmouth College in Hanover, New Hampshire. Already I'd been looking around at several colleges, trying to decide which one was best for me. I liked them all, but Dartmouth impressed me the most. It was a member of the prestigious Ivy League colleges and situated alongside a river, surrounded by groves of elm trees. In particular, at the Thayer School of Engineering, I was delighted to discover its "tool library," where students could check out power tools and batteries as if they were books. Not only that, the machine shop was filled with all kinds of saws and welding kits needed to build just about anything. I couldn't wait to tell Geoffrey and Gilbert.

In addition to science, I also wanted to learn about history and politics, study more languages like French or Mandarin, and perhaps even take courses in painting and acting. I was also encouraged by the number of Africans who attended the college. While touring the campus, I spoke Swahili with a couple of Kenyan engineering students who told me, "Come to Dartmouth, brother. Here you have a family." I'm happy that I took their advice, because the next four years were some of the best of my life.

I won't say that college was easy. Like at ALA, the first year was so challenging that I often got discouraged. At times it was like climbing a sheer cliff, straight up. But with the help of my advisors and tutors, and a lot of time spent studying and reading, my second year got a lot better. By the third year, I was the one helping other students.

But not all of my time was spent in the classroom. At Dartmouth, they believe in learning through projects. And the engineering labs were the greatest places to tinker and experiment. My first year, some classmates and I built a refrigerator that didn't use electricity, but instead an intricate system of water pumps and vacuums. It worked, but never got as cold as we wanted, so I'm still playing around with it.

Another of my favorite projects was a kind of vending machine for charging cell phones. Remember me describing the sidewalk stalls? The problem is they take too much time, and most people are afraid of leaving their phones unattended. The machine we invented allows people to safely lock away devices while they are being charged. First they insert a coin to get a key, which unlocks a personal, phone-sized locker with its own power source. Plug in the phone, lock the cubby, and come back in a couple of hours. Best of all, the machine is powered by solar panels, allowing it to be used anywhere in the world.

Now that it's 2014 and I've graduated from college, people are asking me what I plan to do with my life and where I am going to live. Sure, it would be nice to stay in the States, find a good job in Silicon Valley or New York, and make a lot of money. But that's not me. While I really love the United States, both my heart and life's work belong in Africa. I'll spend another year at the design firm IDEO in San Francisco pursuing an internship so I can learn more about business and design, and after that, I'm going home.

I have a long list of projects I want to start in Malawi,

and several are already under way. After my first appearance at TED, Tom and I started a nonprofit group called Moving Windmills Project to help fund local village improvements and to pay for tuition. Some of the money comes through donations, while the rest I earn by traveling the U.S. and speaking about my life.

One of my main goals for Moving Windmills was to rebuild the schools in my area. As I mentioned earlier, the conditions at both Wimbe Primary and Kachokolo Secondary were terrible. We had no desks, books, or proper supplies. The schools were without electricity and clean water, the windows had no glass to keep out the cold, and the roofs leaked when it rained. Wimbe Primary was built in 1950 and intended for only about 400 students, although more than 1,400 attended when I was a boy. In Malawi, the government only funds certain school buildings, sending their money instead to pay teacher salaries and housing.

So you can imagine how happy I was for Moving Windmills Project to team with an American organization called buildOn.org to help rebuild Wimbe Primary. Based in Stamford, Connecticut, buildOn.org has two parts. The first organizes American high school students to get involved in community service, such as cleaning up neighborhoods, volunteering at homes for the elderly and soup kitchens, tutoring, and so forth. But it also works with communities to help build schools in poor countries across the world. Since 1992, the organization has constructed nearly six hundred schools in Haiti, Nicaragua, Mali, Nepal, Senegal, and Malawi.

We started work on Wimbe in 2010, during one of my school holidays. It was important to have the community involved so that everyone felt they shared in the ownership. Local men made all the bricks, and the rest of the building materials came from within Malawi. As of 2014, we've built four new school blocks with two classrooms each—enough space for over two hundred more students, each with his own desk. And each building is powered with LED lights, solar panels, and deep-cycle batteries, allowing kids and their parents to stay late and study into the night.

Reading is also a lot more fun there. Thanks to the Pearson Foundation, we added ten thousand new books to the library where I first learned about science. Ms. Sikelo now has so many books that she's sharing with other schools in the district.

And as for Kachokolo—people ask me if I'm bitter toward them for kicking me out, but I'm not. In fact, not long ago, I went back and solar-powered the entire compound. We also installed computers connected to a cool program called eGranary, which delivers the wonders of the Internet in places without a network connection. They call it "Internet in a box," and it gives people free access to over three thousand websites, fifty thousand books, and more than one hundred educational and computer software programs. We even hooked it up to a WiFi network, so that everyone in the region with a smartphone can use it 24/7—especially kids who may not be able to afford tuition.

I've now sent most of my sisters to private school. Doris and Aisha are enrolled in college; Doris is studying to become a nurse and Aisha is working toward a degree in rural development. The younger ones are busy learning English and teaching it to their friends. I also helped Gilbert start a small music and film studio in Kasungu.

As for Geoffrey, he's still in Wimbe. His mother fell ill recently and requires his constant help around the house and farm. But this also means he can assist my father, who's busier now than ever. Thanks to my book sales, I founded a small business—a maize mill in Chamama that my family now oversees. And since our farm is producing double the harvests these days, I had to buy two pickups to help carry our crops to market. I'm also trying to start a transportation business, so during my last year at Dartmouth, I ordered a minibus over the Internet from Japan that now moves people up and down Malawi's main highway. My hope is to create the first shuttle service from Kamuzu International Airport in Lilongwe. Right now we have only taxis and dusty minibuses, where you're likely to share your seat with a farmer's goat or chickens.

These businesses are mainly a way to support my family, and they'll do most of the work. Because when I get home, I'll be focused on much bigger things. For one, I'm still dedicated to bringing water and electricity to the rural poor. Already I have designs for easy-to-assemble drills for water wells, along with windmill and battery systems to provide electricity. Not only will they be affordable, but I want to make sure they can also be repaired with simple, everyday materials—such as car parts—so that villages can keep them running.

I hope to make these the flagship projects for an innovation hub I want to open in Lilongwe. It'll be a place where inventors and designers can share and develop ideas, consult with engineers and other professionals in the field, and receive funding. I modeled it after iHub in Nairobi, started by some other TED Fellows, that's been focused on growing Kenya's high-tech community, and to great success. But instead of creating things like software and mobile apps, our hub will use do-it-yourself science and technology to bring Africans access to clean water, electricity, housing, and ways of earning money. The doors will be open to men and women of all ages, but my hope is to attract young students like myself, who might have a great idea but no one to share it with.

By coming back home, I want to inspire the next generation of dreamers.

Young people comprise over half the African population, so the future of the continent hinges upon their energy and ideas and the support we give them. But my story isn't exclusively for them. To the kids elsewhere who are reading this book, whether in Chicago, London, or Beijing, I want you to know that your ambitions are just as important and worth achieving, however big or small. Often people with the best ideas face the greatest challenges—their country at war; a lack of money or education or the support of those around them. But like me, they choose to stay focused because that dream—as far away as it seems—is the truest and most hopeful thing they have. Think of your dreams and ideas as tiny miracle machines inside you that no one can touch. The more faith you put into them, the bigger they get, until one day they'll rise up and take you with them.

ACKNOWLEDGMENTS

To Andrea Barthello & Bill, Sam, Mike, and Ramsay Ritchie—thank you for welcoming me into your family. Your home has always been a refuge from the craziness that is sometimes my life. And to Tom Rielly: When we met, you promised that you'd support me for seven years, no matter what happened. And you kept your promise. What an unforgettable adventure we've had together. As my American parents, you and Andrea provide love, support, and wisdom, for which I will always be grateful. And thanks to my coauthor, Bryan Mealer, who has become like my brother over these years.

To Jackie and Mike Bezos and Eileen and Jay Walker, for your love and support of my education.

To John Collier, Andy Friedland, Karen Gocsik, Brian Reed, Mark Reed, Marcia Calloway, Jim Kim, Carol Harlow, Maria Laskaris, Benjamin Schwartz, and Carrie Fraser—thank you for being on "Team William" and for everything you did to help me achieve my Dartmouth Dream.

To Christopher Schmidt, my tutor and mentor. You

went above and beyond to help me in academics and in life. I graduated from Dartmouth in significant portion due to your efforts.

Thanks to Henry Ferris at HarperCollins for first publishing my book back in 2009, and to Andrea Rosen at the HarperCollins Speaker's Bureau for bringing me the opportunities to earn money to transform my village. Thanks to Lauri Hornik and the wonderful team at Dial Books for helping spread my story to kids of all ages—first a picture book (with the artwork of the talented Elizabeth Zunon) and now a middle-grade edition. And thanks to my agent, Heather Schroder, for both her friendship and tireless work on my behalf. Thanks to Chiwetel Ejiofor for being a friend and fan of my story.

I'm forever grateful to the kind people at TED: Chris Anderson, June Cohen, Bruno Giussani, Emeka Okafor, and the TED Fellows team. TED literally launched me into my new life and made dreams come true that I never knew existed.

And finally, thanks to my friends and family in Malawi for their love, support, and guidance. Thanks to my parents, Agnes and Trywell, and to my sisters Annie, Doris, Aisha, Mayless, Rose, and Tiyamike. I've said it many times and I'll say it again: Your hard work and toughness make me proud of who I am. (Uncle John, Grandpa Matiki, Grandpa and Grandma Kamkwamba, Chief Wimbe, and Khamba—may you all rest in peace!)

To learn more about the
MOVING WINDMILLS PROJECT
and see how you can help,
visit **movingwindmills.org**.